INTERNATIONAL BANK FOR RECONSTRUCTION AND DEVELOPMENT

WORLD BANK STAFF OCCASIONAL PAPERS NUMBER FOUR

D1526597

HANS A. ADLER

SECTOR AND PROJECT PLANNING IN TRANSPORTATION

Distributed by The Johns Hopkins Press
Baltimore and London

FOREWORD

The benefits of research are greater the further they are spread. Because some of the work done within or for the Bank and its affiliated organizations may be useful to others who are engaged in the practice of sound economic development, we have decided to publish papers based on this work from time to time. Most of the papers likely to be published will have an unashamed pragmatic bias, as indeed has the work of the development economist generally. While these papers are published by the Bank, their premises or conclusions are not necessarily accepted by the Bank either in practice or theory; they are entirely the responsibility of the authors. We hope the papers may be a modest stimulus to further research, particularly in the troubled zone where theory meets real life.

George D. Woods
President
International Bank for Reconstruction and Development

TABLE OF CONTENTS

PREFACE

In George Bernard Shaw's *Buoyant Millions,* the father says to his daughter and her fiancé, "you both want to be world betterers, but you don't know enough about the world to run a fish and chip business." The World Bank Group learned very early in its life that bettering the standard of living in a developing country very often begins with bettering its transport system. We also learned that in all countries the transport system is central in any development effort and that efficiency in investment decisions here has wide ramifications.

In its function as an international lender using economic criteria, the Bank has been something of an operating pioneer in the cost-benefit analysis of road, rail, and port projects. Methods have evolved over time, and are still evolving. One of the major tasks is to assess where the project fits within the sector as a whole, not to mention the economy. In some countries, moreover, the project affects the entire transport system.

We hope, by publishing in a compact form these two essays on sector and project planning in transportation by Hans A. Adler, chief transport economist, to help fill a gap in the sparse general literature of the subject. We are grateful to the Brookings Institution for permission to re-publish one of these essays, and pleased to introduce into the series the first publication by a member of the Projects Department of the Bank.

ANDREW M. KAMARCK
Director,
Economics Department

INTERNATIONAL BANK FOR RECONSTRUCTION AND DEVELOPMENT

WORLD BANK STAFF OCCASIONAL PAPERS NUMBER FOUR

I

PREPARING TRANSPORT SECTOR PROGRAMS

INTRODUCTION

Importance of Transport Planning

The preparation of programs for the transportation sector of developing countries is an infant industry which has been growing rapidly in recent years. The World Bank, which is probably the organization most actively engaged in the administration of transport surveys both on its own account and as executing agency for the United Nations Development Programme, participated in about twenty such surveys in the three-year period from 1964 to 1966, and in early 1967 had under consideration six more. Other transportation surveys are being undertaken with the assistance of the United States, France, the United Kingdom, Germany and other countries and international agencies. In only a few instances are developing countries attempting surveys without outside assistance.

The impetus for these surveys comes primarily from three sources. First, there is an increasing recognition that macro-economic planning is not enough and that it urgently needs the support of detailed analyses of individual projects. Project analysis alone, however, is frequently not sufficient because in the transportation sector there tends to be a close interrelationship among individual projects; for example, the success of a particular railway investment may depend on whether or not a competing road is improved; the effectiveness of a port investment may depend not only on improvements in competing ports but also on rail and road connections to the port; and the justification for a road improvement may depend on what is done to parallel or feeder roads. The function of the sector program is, therefore, to identify promising projects, to relate them properly to one another, to determine their priorities, and to relate all projects together properly to the macro-economic plan.

A second reason for transport surveys arises from the fact that the transportation systems of most countries are severely distorted due to historical circumstances. Probably the single most important factor is the collapse of the monopoly which railways had for almost a century and the consequent painful adjustments of the railways to vigorous competition by road transport. Many governments tried to avoid or postpone the needed changes which the rise of road transport inevitably called for (such as relating tariffs more closely to costs and abandoning uneconomic railway lines), but in so doing they seriously distorted the transport system and made the final adjustments all the more agonizing.

A third and more mundane reason for the increase in the number of transport sector surveys in developing countries is the insistence on them by foreign governments and international organizations providing financial assistance, who want to assure themselves that the projects they finance are justified and have a high priority. This can be determined only by establishing the position of the project in the sector as a whole. These three reasons—the recognition that macro-economic planning and project analysis alone are not sufficient, the distortions in transportation, and the insistence of foreign aid givers—are, of course, interrelated.

The preparation of transport programs is particularly important because in developing countries a transport infrastructure is usually a prerequisite—though by no means a guarantee—of economic growth. In addition, transport requirements tend to grow at a considerably higher rate than national income in the early stages of development. In a dozen Asian countries for example, the annual increase in rail and road traffic in the 1950's ranged from about 6 to 20 per cent, while national income was growing at from 2 to 5 per cent. It is thus not unusual for traffic growth to be two or even four times as large as the rise in economic activity. As a result, and because the ratio of capital to output is high for transport especially in its early stages, investments in transportation often account for a large part of public investment. Their share is frequently as much as 15 to 30 per cent; in the Honduras 1965-69 plan, it was as high as 37 per cent. Transport investments in the private sector also tend to be sizeable; in Pakistan's 1965-70 plan, private transport investments, primarily for motor vehicles, account for 17 per cent of total private investments.

The importance of transport investments is enhanced by the fact that a significant part of these investments in developing countries involves foreign exchange expenditures. The extent of this varies, depending primarily on the degree of a country's industrialization and the type of investment. In both Colombia and Chile, for example, the foreign exchange component of transport investments in the 1960's has been estimated at more than 40 per cent, in Ecuador at about 50 per cent, in Syria at nearly 60 per cent, and in Nepal as high as 75 per cent. In addition, a new investment's operating costs also tend to include continuing foreign exchange expenditures on spare parts, maintenance equipment, tires and fuel.

Transport sector planning is also important, especially in developing countries, because governments own or control nearly all transport facilities. Railways, roads, ports, inland waterways, airfields and airlines tend to be exclusively public investments and the major private investments, such as motor vehicles, are usually controlled by production licenses, import restrictions and foreign exchange controls. Governments therefore generally have the instruments to ensure that the program can be carried out. On the other hand, transportation is exposed to the threat of political interference, which can make planning based on economic criteria a wasted effort. Sound economic analysis may be helpful against political pressures.

Conditions for a Transport Survey

There are three important conditions which should be met before a transport survey is undertaken. The first relates to an understanding of the broad transport policies which a government plans to pursue; the second concerns the steps which are needed to ensure that the survey becomes an effective "kick-off" to continuous planning; and the third, which is discussed in the section on traffic forecasting, deals with planning in other sectors.

The uneconomic use of government-owned transportation facilities for defense, political and social purposes is sometimes so extensive that the World Bank has on occasion agreed to participate in transport surveys only after reaching an understanding with the government on the broad transport policies to be followed. This is most important for the operation of railways because the collapse of their former monopoly position has created special difficulties for them and because they are particularly subject to governmental interferences. Major issues may include the following: is the railway management to be given full responsibility over day-to-day operations, and government intervention limited to such broad policy issues as the size of new investments and major changes in tariff levels? Will the railway be permitted to dismiss redundant workers and eliminate uneconomic lines and stations? Will new lines be constructed only if detailed studies indicate that the lines are economically justified? Should tariff policy aim at the principle that rates and fares should be sufficient to cover at least the marginal costs of transporting each commodity and each type of passenger traffic, and the full costs of carrying the traffic as a whole?

A transportation study of Argentina, for example, found that of a total railway network of about 43,000 km, about 14,000 km of lines, or about one-third of the entire network, were uneconomic

6

and should be abandoned, that an additional 5,000 km needed further study with an eye to possible later abandonment, and that the labor force could be reduced by 30,000-40,000, or by about 15-20 per, cent. It is, of course, no use to study these problems if for political or other reasons the government is not in a position to do anything about them. Brazil has been building many new lines, most of them uneconomic, for allegedly defense purposes; unless the government is either willing to stop the construction of lines that a study would show to be uneconomic or to treat them as a defense expenditure, financed from the defense budget, an economic study would be of little use. Similarly, revenues of the Brazilian Federal Railways have in recent years covered only between one-third and one-half of operating expenditures; there is no point in studying the difficult measures needed to bring revenues in line with costs unless the government is prepared to face the complex political and social problems involved in carrying out these measures. Brazil did face these issues squarely before beginning a comprehensive transport survey, though it is too early to judge whether it will ultimately carry out its intentions. In this connection, while it is of course true that the detailed measures cannot be known until the survey is completed, the major problems and the broad solutions are nearly always identifiable well in advance.

A second condition for undertaking a transport survey is the recognition by the government concerned that planning is not a one-shot affair but a continuous process. Too many transport programs have been prepared by international consultants who visited a country for several months or even a year, and who left behind nothing but a well-bound report. Such a report may help attract foreign lending and may even stimulate a new awareness of certain problems and their solutions, but however sound the program may be, its preparation is hardly worth the effort unless it can serve as an effective "kick-off" to continuous planning, increasingly undertaken by local experts themselves without foreign assistance.

That this point must be made at all is somewhat surprising because it has always been fully recognized for macro-economic planning. Few, if any, sensible governments have permitted their over-all economic plans to be prepared by outsiders without local counterparts, and in most cases the former have only served as advisors to a national planning organization. There may be certain reasons why this has frequently not been the case in transportation planning, such as the greater interest of economists in macro-economic planning and the resultant shortage of transport economists. Nevertheless, if the survey is to have lasting value, every effort should be made to train local experts to staff a permanent planning organization.

One of the most effective ways of achieving this objective is the creation of a counterpart organization, so that each of the foreign technicians works with at least one local counterpart. This has several important advantages. First, it provides effective, on-the-spot training, and thus lays the basis for future planning with progressively less foreign assistance. Second, it creates a local team of experts familiar with the program and the reasons for its recommendations, and able to assist in its implementation and modification. And third, counterparts can help the foreign experts who are usually less familiar than they with the particular conditions of the country, the history and background of certain problems, the sources of information and the details of government organization. The participation of local counterparts in the preparation of the program should be supplemented with continuing—but decreasing —assistance by foreign advisors for several years thereafter, and with the training of local experts abroad. The importance of the training aspects is now increasingly recognized and the United Nations Development Programme has made it a practice to finance training as part of its assistance for transport surveys.

Brazil provides an example of an effective transport planning organization in a developing country. Brazil had neglected transport planning for many years and found itself by 1964 in a situation in which an inefficient and costly transport system, with large deficits, was contributing materially to runaway inflation and balance of payments difficulties and was undermining the country's agricultural and industrial development. The government recognized that a thorough study of these problems was essential and called upon the World Bank for assistance. After agreement had been reached with the Bank on certain basic transport policies, terms of reference for the studies were drawn up and international consultants were selected. In the meantime, the government made vigorous efforts to recruit Brazilian counterparts. A separate agency was set up for this purpose which, under dynamic leadership and with considerable latitude in recruitment, interviewed and tested several hundred applicants for their technical knowledge, language ability and psychological attitude toward working with foreigners. In this way, about eighty Brazilian counterparts were selected who worked full time with the foreign experts on the transport studies. As a result, Brazil is beginning to develop a core of transport experts who will be able to continue transport planning with progressively less foreign assistance. It should be emphasized, however, that this successful effort was essentially a crash program to meet a crisis situation, and it remains to be seen whether future governments will give economic development a sufficiently high priority to ensure a continuous, institutionalized planning effort.

Scope of Program

The scope of transport programs can vary widely. The most typical—and generally the most desirable—program covers a country's entire transport system, including all modes of transport. An exception is urban transportation which has its own unique problems and is to a considerable extent separable from the inter-city and rural transport network. Nevertheless, urban transport must be considered for total vehicle requirements, and to the extent that it affects intercity traffic, e.g. where urban congestion interferes with adequate access to a port, or where bypasses are needed.

Some programs are less broad. In India and Brazil, for example, the size of the country and the complexity of the transport system made it impractical to prepare programs which would cover the entire country at once. These countries were, therefore, divided into regions, with the idea of ultimately building up a country-wide program from the individual regional ones. Some programs do not cover all modes; a program for Argentina, for example, excluded aviation, and one for Honduras was limited to roads. This is

9

usually undesirable, though the practical consequences may not always be serious, depending primarily on the degree to which substitution between modes is possible.

Many transport programs do not include, at least in detail, feeder roads intended to open up new land for agricultural development or otherwise closely related to an agricultural project. In these cases roads are a joint cost with other investments and the realization of benefits depends not only on the road, but also on these investments, as well as on such other measures as land reform, extension services, etc. The planning of feeder roads is, therefore, handled more effectively in agricultural surveys rather than in transport surveys. Transport programs do, however, frequently include general financial allowances for such roads.

More recently a number of studies have been undertaken which cover not only one country but several. For example, a transport survey of Central America in 1965 included five countries, and several studies in Africa are also on a multi-national basis. This is particularly important where major traffic flows go beyond the border of one country, such as those of landlocked countries like Chad and Bolivia where the transport facilities of one country are closely interlinked with those of its neighbor, such as the Mali and Senegal railways or where attempts to form a common market will change the pattern of traffic and transport investments, as in Central America. As emphasized below, transport programs, regardless of their geographic or modal scope, should in all cases deal not only with new investments but also with the measures needed to make the optimum use of existing investments.

Basic Steps in Methodology

The preparation of a transport program can be divided into five distinct, though interrelated, steps. The first is to identify the basic goals which are being sought, such as promoting economic development in the country as a whole or in specific regions, creating employment opportunities and ensuring the efficient utilization of scarce resources—including especially capital and foreign exchange—and the country's general strategy for achieving these goals. Second, it is necessary to prepare an inventory of the existing transport facilities, their condition and utilization. Third, a forecast of traffic must be made and the traffic then distributed to each mode of transport. Fourth, transport policies and operations must be examined to determine to what extent improvements can make it possible to carry future traffic at minimum cost. And finally, a detailed program must be prepared identifying new investments and their priorities. Each one of these steps will be discussed separately below; the terms of reference for a representative type of transport survey are given in the Annex.

OBJECTIVES OF THE PROGRAM

Since transportation is a service designed to connect production and population centers with each other or with consumption centers, transportation cannot be said to have a separate objective independent of a country's developmental goals. If, for example, a country has mineral resources which it wants to develop for export, the necessary railway and port investments are essentially a joint cost together with the mining investments, and the justification for the transport investment hinges essentially on the justification for the project as a whole. The same would be true for feeder roads to promote new agricultural production. If a country wants to discourage excessively crowded cities, transport policies and investments in urban areas must be properly related to such a goal. If the emphasis is on the development of heavy industry, the railways play an important role; if it is on light industry and production of consumer goods, the use of trucking becomes more crucial. A country's general strategy for economic development thus dictates the appropriate transport strategy, though the former must, of course, take into account transport costs as one of the relevant factors. This is one of the important reasons why the best time for initiating a transport survey is when programs are also being prepared for other sectors.

Within this broader context, the objective of transport planning is to ensure that the traffic will be carried at the lowest cost to

11

the economy. The concept of "lowest cost" involves complexities which are discussed below in connection with the distribution of traffic among the transport modes.

It is one of the important facts of transport life that governments use transport services extensively to subsidize a variety of social, political and defense objectives through rates and fares below cost. In some countries, all railway passenger traffic is subsidized while in others specific groups such as the military, school children, government officials, priests or commuters pay especially low fares. Sometimes most freight is subsidized, while in other cases the subsidy is limited to certain commodities, specific distances of haul, or branch line traffic. Aviation tends to be subsidized to promote a country's political integration or its international prestige. While some of these subsidies are the result of conscious government decisions, many are quite inadvertent because costs are not known or because of a general reluctance to raise tariffs.

There may, indeed, be a limited role for subsidies to transportation. For example, new transport systems may deserve support as a form of infant industry, as in the case of aviation in its early stage. There may also be individual instances where the promotion of transport *per se*—rather than of increased production or consumption of goods or other services—is a legitimate goal, as where a country's social and political integration can be promoted in this way. On the other hand, while a government may have an interest in promoting transport, it can hardly have a legitimate interest in promoting the less efficient transport alternative; i.e. it is not economically justified in using a particular transport mode as the subsidy device if the same goal can be achieved at lower cost through another mode or a non-transportation alternative. This may seem quite obvious, but the vehement objection to abandoning railway lines when the traffic can be carried more efficiently on parallel roads indicates that its application is often difficult.

Moreover, even if the social, political and defense objectives deserve government support, subsidized transportation is a particularly inefficient method for achieving them. There are several

12

important reasons for this. First, the subsidy is in effect hidden and its amount is difficult to ascertain since allocating transport costs to specific users is a complex task, subject to wide margins of error and disagreement. Indeed, the fact that the subsidy is hidden is one of the reasons why this device is politically so attractive; it may also explain why so often no action is taken to change the subsidy. Second, the subsidy usually has to be financed by charging prices higher than costs for other transport services; this was possible for the railways when they still had a monopoly position but has become increasingly less feasible with the growth of road transport, and has contributed to the difficulties of railways in meeting road competition. Passenger subsidies are frequently financed by charging higher rates for freight—either for bulk commodities, whose transportation is essential for the country's industrial growth, or for general cargo, whose shift to road transport is thus needlessly accelerated. (It is interesting that in the Soviet Union, profits on passenger services have helped to subsidize freight traffic, which is in sharp contrast to the practice in most countries.)

Third, transport subsidies tend, in effect, to support indiscriminately a multitude of diverse activities ranging from business functions, vacations and social visits to religious pilgrimages; these hardly deserve equal government support and, if openly avowed, would rarely receive it. Fourth, using a particular transport mode for subsidization leads to distortions between modes; inadequate road user charges, for example, tend to shift traffic to roads even though it might be more efficiently carried by railway. Fifth, transport subsidies distort the location of new industries or population, and discourage existing industries from moving to more economic locations. If, for example, the charges for carrying coal or iron ore are subsidized, steel mills tend to be located where they impose a heavier burden on the transport system; if charges are above transport costs, other locational advantages will be given up to reduce transportation costs. Sixth, passenger transport subsidization is frequently inconsistent with policies aiming at a more equal income distribution since the people who can afford to travel are usually in the middle and upper classes. Finally, it is sometimes argued that keeping transport prices low, regardless of costs, helps

13

to reduce inflation in countries confronted with this problem. This may be valid in the short run for psychological reasons, but it merely increases government deficits, which are at least as inflationary as higher transport prices.

Instead of using the transport system as a subsidy device, it would be much more efficient to have the responsible government agencies finance the subsidy directly through their own budgets, either by supporting the ultimate objective directly or by buying the transport service at commercial rates. If, for example, a government deems it desirable to have school children become familiar with their country, the Ministry of Education should buy the necessary transport services and be responsible for justifying the expenditures involved; similarly, if a country wants to promote the production of iron ore, direct payments to producers are more efficient than hidden transport subsidies. It is not surprising that many of these objectives look much less important to the interested government agencies when they have to finance and justify them directly in their own budgets than when they can impose the costs on others. Even the promotion of employment, which is certainly an important goal in developing countries, can be achieved more efficiently by appropriate wage and investment policies than by insisting that the railway hire thousands of workers which it does not need; this merely disguises the underlying situation without really improving it.

TRANSPORT INVENTORY

Most developing countries do not have adequate, up-to-date and readily accessible information about their transport system. It is obvious that without a clear idea of the quantity and quality of existing facilities and their utilization, rational planning for future requirements is hardly possible.

The preparation of an inventory of available facilities, and of their condition and utilization is, therefore, essential. It is a time-consuming job, which can account for as much as one-half of the effort involved in preparing a transport program. In the case of a

14

transport survey of the Eastern Region of India, for example, making the basic inventory alone took more than a year; this is unusual and was largely explained by the complexity of the region and the limited information which was initially available.

The inventory should cover not only the physical facilities, but should also indicate the degree of their utilization, the volume and composition of traffic flows, the costs of transport and the related tariffs, the financial situation of transport enterprises, and the government's transport policies. Such an inventory can be prepared most readily for railways and other transport entities which are operated on commercial lines and have appropriate accounting and statistical systems. Most railways have at least some information on their facilities and rolling stock (including type, condition and utilization), on traffic carried, on over-all costs and tariffs, and on their financial condition. However, in the case of many railways the data are incomplete. Few railways, for example, have sufficient information on the origin and destination of much of their traffic, or on traffic by individual lines, on the cost of carrying different types of traffic (commodities as well as passengers) by individual lines, on the replacement cost of assets at present values, and on maintenance costs of various equipment. In addition, the available data are all too often inaccurate. For example, an intensive study of the traffic on branch lines of the Spanish Railway indicated that the traffic on some of them was less than one-half of that indicated in the official statistics. The traffic of one of Brazil's major railways in a recent year was found to be about 2 billion ton/km (or about 15 per cent) less than that given in its official statistics. The inaccuracies in statistics reflect the fact that they are not used sufficiently by the management in planning, so that errors do not come to light until someone—usually an outsider—wants to use the data.

For aviation, ports and ocean shipping, the situation is similar to railways, but reliable information on inland shipping and roads and road transport is even rarer. Most countries have a general idea of the length of their road network and how much of it is paved, but few have an inventory which describes the condition of

15

the roads, their width, grades, curvature, capacity and traffic, all of which are necessary for intelligent planning. The preparation of a road inventory, even excluding information on traffic, is time-consuming; an experienced team (consisting of a highway engineer, a surveyor and an assistant) may be able to cover 1,000-1,500 miles per month, depending on road conditions. This means that for a country like Colombia, with about 20,000 miles of roads, it would take three teams about half a year. Similarly, it is essential to have an inventory of the motor vehicle fleet by type, capacity, age, operating costs, etc. In many countries such information is available only with large margins of error.

The collection of road traffic information is unusually complex. Many developing countries have begun only recently to make traffic counts, and these are generally available for only one or two past years, for a few days during the year and at a few locations which may not be representative. A proper traffic inventory should at least provide information on major commodities and passengers carried, their origin and destination, the type of vehicle, its capacity and load factor. Because traffic may vary widely during the day, the week and the seasons of the year, it is necessary to get hourly and daily traffic data, as well as enough information on seasonal variations to make reasonable estimates of annual traffic. Only after the existing traffic pattern has been established is it possible to estimate future traffic.

FORECASTING TRAFFIC

Estimating future traffic is still an imprecise—but essential—art. Since transport investments commonly have long lives, many as long as twenty years or more, decisions to make such investments inherently involve long-term forecasts. It is clearly preferable to be explicit about the underlying assumptions than to leave them unstated.

Traffic forecasting falls into three main stages. The first involves an estimate of the volume and location of future agricultural, industrial and mining output and its consumption, including also

16

exports and imports; an analogous estimate is needed for population volume and location. The second stage requires translating output and population data into traffic, both by volume and by origin and destination. And finally, the traffic must be distributed to the transport mode which can carry it most efficiently. The three steps are interrelated since regional outputs and traffic flows depend in part on transport costs.

Since future traffic depends on developments in the industrial, agricultural, mining and other sectors of the economy, and on population developments, traffic forecasts can be no better than forecasts of developments in these areas. Unfortunately, it is not sufficient to estimate output merely in macro-economic terms, since such transport investments as roads, railway lines and ports are fixed at definite locations and cannot be moved to other areas. It is therefore necessary to estimate not merely future production and consumption as a whole, but also its specific location. For mobile equipment, such as motor vehicles and railway rolling stock, this refinement is less necessary.

The need for specific, long-term traffic forecasts implies that in the absence of planning in other sectors, transport planning is of only limited usefulness. For example, Malaysia recently contemplated preparing a twenty-year transport plan based on specific projects and their priorities. For investments having a life of twenty years, this would have required traffic forecasts for forty years from the present for the investments to be made toward the end of the twenty-year period. Since such long-range planning did not exist in other sectors, and since it would in any case not have been very meaningful, it would not have been a useful exercise for transportation. In general, therefore, transport plans should be limited to about ten years—five years in detail and an additional five years in less detail. Macro-economic planning should, of course, have a longer horizon and beyond the ten-year period might well include expenditures under projects previously started, projects which were reviewed for the ten-year program but found to be premature, and global estimates of transport requirements on a macro-economic basis; this is in fact the type of perspective program which Malaysia decided to prepare (see Annex). The best time for undertaking a transport survey is when planning is also going on for other sectors, as was done, for example, in the case of Ecuador's 1964-73 plan and Korea's 1967-72 plan. This will permit the optimum integration of transport requirements with those of other sectors.

After estimates have been made of future production and consumption, these must be translated into traffic. This is generally done on the basis of past relationships between output and consumption and traffic requirements, with adjustments for foreseeable future changes, such as a possible decline in the railway's share of certain traffic, changes in relative costs, etc. Recently attempts have been made to build transportation models, which are an expression of the mathematical relationships between the magnitude of traffic-generating factors and the volume of the resulting traffic. Unfortunately, the factors are frequently complex and the construction of the model difficult and time-consuming. For example, an initial model for coal transportation in the Eastern Region of India was able to explain only about one-half of the actual coal traffic. One difficulty was that coal is not a homogeneous commodity so that it had to be broken down into various types, such as coking and non-coking coal; another problem arose from the fact that some of the coal originating from captive mines was not being moved in accordance with the lowest distribution costs because these mines evidently offered certain advantages, such as the assured availability of supplies, which offset the higher transport costs. It would no doubt have been possible to build a model allowing for these factors, but this would have required substantially more time and staff than was available. A related problem arose in a transport survey of Central America where the model indicated impossibly high increases in future air traffic; the difficulty was that the value of passenger time, which is an essential ingredient in aviation demand, was not known and the value used was based on inapplicable U.S. experience. In both the Indian and the Central American cases it became necessary to proceed with the more standard techniques of reliance on past traffic trends adjusted for specific new developments in sight. Nevertheless, as indicated above, such models can be useful tools and even when they fail may reveal interesting lessons; they will no doubt be used increasingly in the future.

The final step is to estimate the division of traffic among the various transport modes. In principle, the traffic should be allocated to the particular mode which can carry it at lowest cost. In this connection, three special problems deserve mention. First, determining costs is frequently difficult because of inadequate data and because the relevant costs are those to the economy, which may differ from private, financial costs. The types of adjustments necessary, primarily in the prices for labor, capital and foreign exchange, are discussed more fully in the second article. Second, traffic will in practice not move via the low cost carrier if the rates charged do not reflect transport costs. This is frequently the case, especially for railways, where rates take into account the value of the commodity and tend to be uniform among lines in spite of cost differences. User charges for roads and ports also rarely reflect costs properly. The transport survey should indicate the resultant distortions and recommend the steps needed to eliminate them.

A third difficulty arises from the fact that there are important qualitative differences between the various transport modes; some of these are difficult to quantify, so that it is not easy to determine the lowest costs when these differences are taken into account. Road transport, for example, provides a door-to-door service, usually with substantial savings in time compared to railway service, greater frequency and reliability, lower breakage and losses, quicker settlement of claims and other similar advantages. This is particularly important for general cargo and accounts for a major part of the trend to road transport, even though the direct transport costs by road may in fact be higher than rail costs. It is important to keep in mind that the ultimate aim is not lowest transport cost but lowest cost for the delivered goods; these two are not always the same. The neglect of these total distribution costs in some surveys accounts for unduly optimistic forecasts for rail and coastal shipping potentials and underestimates for road transport. For passenger traffic, too, there are not only differences in transport costs, but also in time, comfort and convenience and probability of accident.

There are fortunately a number of practical considerations which make long-term traffic forecasting more manageable than might appear at first sight. First, a major part of the traffic of many railways and ports consists of only a few bulk commodities, such as coal, ores and grain, so that the analysis can be largely limited to these. Second, many transport investments are relatively lumpy. A port berth might be justified for 80,000 tons of general cargo per year, but might also handle efficiently 150,000 tons, so that a refinement of whether the traffic will be 80,000 or 125,000 tons may not be needed; for bulk cargo, the range might be as much as 300,000 to 1 million tons or even more. Similarly, a paved two-lane road may handle as many as 5,000 vehicles per day, so that estimates of 3,000 or 4,000 vehicles may still lead to the same investment. On the other hand, lumpiness presents a particularly difficult issue if the traffic forecast is at the margin of, say, one or two berths or a two- or four-lane road. For this and other reasons it is important to try to reduce the consequences of lumpiness by, for example, stage construction of roads.

Third, much of the future traffic, especially in the short and medium term, is traffic which exists already, and basic patterns in the location of industry, agriculture and population do not tend to change drastically overnight.

Fourth, in many cases the forecast need only be made until the time when traffic reaches the project's capacity, provided it can be assumed that traffic will not decline thereafter; this is frequently the case, especially for roads. Fifth, because future benefits are discounted by opportunity costs of capital, which in developing countries tend to be as high as 10 or 12 per cent, the correctness of forecasts in the more distant future is substantially less important than it would be at lower discount rates. Finally, because transport, and especially road transport, is nearly always very dynamic in developing countries, an overestimate of traffic might be made up a short time later, so that the cost of the mistake would be less than if the estimated traffic level were never reached. From this point of view, investments in railway lines tend to be much riskier because traffic for most railways has been growing less rapidly than for roads, while the life of railway track and equipment tends to be very long.

TRANSPORT POLICIES AND OPERATIONS

Many transport programs neglect to make a thorough review of transport policies and operations to ensure the efficient utilization of existing investments and to minimize the need for new ones. This is particularly important for developing countries in view of their serious shortage of capital, the large requirements for transport investments and the heavy foreign exchange component of these investments.

Transport Policies

In few sectors of the economy are archaic and wasteful policies as prevalent as in transportation. Some of the most important policies, therefore, which a transport survey should examine include the following:

(a) *The rationality of the criteria used in deciding on new investments.* Few countries base transport investments on the systematic application of cost-benefit techniques; where such studies are made they tend to have such deficiencies as the use of low financial interest rates instead of the higher economic (opportunity) cost of capital, the failure to take into account alternative road transport when building a new railway line, or vice versa, chronic underestimation of costs, and innumerable others. A related problem is the continued maintenance of old investments even though other modes or facilities are more economic, as for example, in the case of uneconomic railway lines and parallel roads. Appropriate transport investment criteria are the subject of the second article.

(b) *The relationship of tariffs to costs.* An efficient allocation of funds to transportation compared to other sectors, and an

21

optimum distribution of traffic among competing transport modes, require that rates and fares reflect the costs of the principal categories of traffic handled—not only for the network as a whole but also by individual line. The survey should, therefore, identify tariffs above and below costs of major traffic categories, the resultant distortions in traffic and investments, and whether adequate freedom exists in fixing and adjusting tariffs. Because the charges for public transport in many developing countries are frequently below cost, transport unfortunately tends to be a serious drain on public savings. This is an area where much can be learned from Soviet practice, where the railways, for example, make substantial contributions to the government budget, in addition to financing the expansion of railway capacity.

(c) *The adequacy of user charges.* In most developing countries, governments do not charge the users of roads, ports, airports, etc., adequately for the cost of these services through fuel taxes, license fees, tolls or other charges. In most Latin American countries, for example, the users of roads pay for less than half of road costs. As in the case of subsidized tariffs, this is likely to lead to distortions between different transport modes, over-investment in transport as a whole, inefficient location of new industries, and an undue burden on the tax system and on public savings, which are particularly serious bottlenecks in nearly all developing countries.

(d) *The nature of the regulatory system.* The transport survey should also review governmental policies on the regulation of trucking and bus services, including licensing, route and distance restrictions, limitations on rates and fares, and weight, and other controls, as well as their enforcement. Many developing countries have inherited the regulatory systems developed in Europe and the United States to protect railway monopolies or to meet the special problems of the depression of the 1930's, even though these systems have little application to the usually very different transport problems of developing countries. The distortions from generally limiting trucks to short hauls of 40 miles, as in New Zealand, or to intrastate traffic, as in the past in India, can lead to a substantial waste of resources.

22

(e) *Other policies* which should be reviewed include: (i) whether taxes, including import duties, are neutral among the various transport modes; (ii) whether the government discriminates in the availability and terms of financing among the modes; (iii) whether the government tries to allocate traffic directly to a specific mode; (iv) whether the government controls the production or imports of vehicles, spare parts, etc. in a way which discriminates against a particular mode; and (v) whether the government imposes any special responsibility on a particular mode without adequate compensation.

Because governments can develop and administer their transport policies only when properly organized to do so, a transport survey must also review the institutional arrangements. It must ask whether a central transport organization exists at all, and if so, analyze the scope of its authority, i.e. whether it includes all modes and methods of coordination, whether it is properly staffed, and whether adequate statistics are available, so that policies can be established and applied intelligently.

Transport Operations

The opportunities for minimizing the need for new investments by operational improvements are usually very extensive, especially for railways and ports, but also for roads. Such improvements relate to all phases of operations, from the better utilization of rolling stock and other equipment to the better maintenance of roads, better labor practices, modern accounting and statistical systems, and appropriate organizational arrangements and administrative procedures.

A few examples will serve to illustrate the importance of this. The Brazilian Federal Railways had intended to spend about $80 million in rolling stock during a recent three-year period. This investment had been based on a traffic forecast and assumed more or less the prevailing operational practices. However, a review of these practices indicated that productivity could be drastically increased. For example, 25 per cent of the diesel locomotives were out of use when better maintenance facilities could have reduced

23

this to less than 10 per cent; the utilization of serviceable diesels was only about 70 per cent, as against the 85 per cent common in other countries; the average turn-around time of freight cars was about thirteen days, when eight days would have been a reasonable goal; the average speed of most trains was less than 14 miles per hour, when better operations in stations and yards, better track conditions and signalling equipment might have increased this to perhaps 20 miles; because of the seasonal nature of agricultural production, the Railways had considerable excess capacity in the off seasons, even though more silos and other storage facilities might have reduced the extremes of seasonal transport requirements; and trains were generally short because station platforms and marshalling yards had never been enlarged. What the Railways really needed was not large new investments in rolling stock but measures to improve the utilization of existing stock. It was estimated that with such improvements it would be possible to reduce rolling stock requirements by about $50 million, though it was, of course, necessary to increase other investments, such as line and terminal improvements. Not only would this permit a saving of about $15 million in new investments, but the return on investments would also be higher. Brazil's is an extreme example but it does illustrate the type of problem common to many railways.

The absence of adequate accounting and statistical systems is a serious drawback for efficient utilization of investments. Few railways in developing countries have sufficient information, for example, on the maintenance costs of old rolling stock to determine the optimum time for replacing it with new equipment. Similarly, few highway departments have reliable information on maintenance costs of different types of road.

The operational problems of many ports are especially acute. At some berths of the port of Calcutta, for example, wheat is unloaded by bagging it on board ship, unloading it, and then emptying the bags in order to transport the wheat by rail in bulk. As a result the unloading rate per day is about 1,000 tons per ship, compared to 4,000-6,000 tons at other Indian ports using mechanical unloading facilities. Port inefficiencies are particularly costly to developing

24

countries because of their frequently heavy dependence on exports and imports.

Organizational and administrative arrangements are also frequently unsatisfactory. Many railways do not have adequate authority over day-to-day operations; highway departments may be saddled with responsibility for other public works; the various port activities, such as pilotage, tug assistance, loading and unloading, customs, storage and inland transport are often not properly integrated; and probably no country in the world has an effective organization for the coordination of the various transport modes. It is essential, therefore, that before new investments are considered, every effort should be made to achieve the optimum utilization of existing ones.

THE INVESTMENT PROGRAM

Once future traffic patterns have been estimated and the opportunities for policy and operational improvements have been taken into account, the next step is to decide on the new investments needed to carry the traffic efficiently. For this purpose it is conceptually useful to divide investments into three basic types because the economic analysis is different for each of them: investments needed to increase capacity, those to replace old equipment with similar but new equipment, and those necessary for modernization, where new and different equipment is substituted for existing equipment, regardless of age.

While these types of investment are, of course, interrelated, the historical pattern of railway investments in many countries indicates that the distinction is a useful one. In the United States, for example, the history of railway investments can be divided into three stages. In the initial period, which lasted until the end of the 19th century, most of the investments were to increase track and other capacity; thereafter, until World War I, investment in rolling stock became relatively more important. After 1920, railway passenger traffic declined drastically, freight traffic increased only modestly, and the railway network was reduced by almost 40,000 miles so that net investments did not increase significantly. These developments were also reflected in the ratio of total capital to output, which decreased progressively from about 16 in 1880 to 6 at the turn of the century, to 4 in the 1920's and to less than 3 in the 1950's; the marginal capital to output ratio declined from about 10 before 1890 to -0.2 in 1927-50. In the early period, large indivisible investments were made, which were only gradually completed; once the basic network existed, output was free to expand with relatively little additional investment.

This pattern of investments is also relevant for developing countries. In Argentina and Brazil, for example, hardly any new investments are needed to increase railway capacity; on the contrary, capacity is generally excessive and investments are only required for replacement and modernization. The Indian Railways, on the other hand, still require large increases in capacity and, within the limited resources available, have to give lower priority to investments for modernization.

In road construction, too, the first investments are to create capacity, but after a basic network exists the major effort consists of improving it. Paving a gravel road is a form a modernization, but also increases capacity. As for road vehicles, the initial effort must be to create a minimum fleet. In the early stages of the growth of the fleet, replacement tends to be only a small part of total investments in vehicles because they are used for long periods—in India, for example, as much as twenty years. Such long periods may partly be explained by the high capital costs, while maintenance costs are relatively low due to the large labor component. As these relationships change, vehicles are replaced earlier and replacement becomes an increasing proportion of total investment. Finally, in more developed countries, the obsolescence of vehicles may at times become more important as a cause for replacement than growing maintenance costs.

Investments to expand capacity are most directly related to increases in freight and passenger traffic, so these can be translated readily into rolling stock requirements, additional port berths, or aircraft. Because of fluctuations in demand, such as those caused by seasonal variations in agricultural output, there is inevitably excess capacity during some parts of the year. Furthermore, if demand is larger than forecast and if capacity cannot be quickly expanded, there is the danger that transport may become a bottleneck to economic growth. This happened, for example, in India in the early 1960's when the railway was unable to carry all of the coal output. To calculate the proper level of reserve capacity requires a delicate balancing of the extra costs involved and the costs of not being able to carry some freight at all or at higher cost and thus slowing down economic development. On the other hand, if the demand for passenger traffic is artificially stimulated by subsidized fares, it may be appropriate to meet with new investments only the demand which would exist at fares which would cover costs. Such a policy, by permitting congestion, would equalize the value of the service and the fare charged. The problem of excess capacity is perhaps less serious for road transport because of the greater flexibility of the vehicle fleet, the availability of alternative roads and the fact that most roads in developing countries operate far below physical capacity, though increased traffic may involve congestion costs. Traffic and capacity are, of course, interrelated: while traffic determines capacity, capacity and related costs determine traffic. In too many surveys, the latter relationship is neglected.

The second type of investment is to replace old equipment with similar but new equipment. The proper timing of such replacement depends primarily on two types of factors: first, the capital costs of new equipment minus the scrap value of old equipment, and the relative costs of maintaining them, including both the direct costs and the costs of nonutilization during maintenance, which tend to increase with age: and second, obsolescence, i.e. the availability of new equipment incorporating technological improvements.

The proper timing of replacement investments is by no means the same for different countries. The labor component of maintaining freight cars, for example, is substantially greater than of producing new cars. In countries with low wages and a high oppor-

27

tunity cost of capital, replacement should take place later than in more developed countries. This is, in fact, what happens. For example, a study of the optimum age for replacing freight cars in India indicates that it is somewhere between forty and forty-five years; a similar analysis for New Zealand indicates it to be no more than thirty-five years.

The third type of investment is for modernization of facilities or equipment which have become obsolete because technological improvements or other radical changes have taken place. For example, in the replacement of steam locomotives, the relevant comparison is no longer between the capital and operating costs of new and those of old steam engines, but with the costs of diesel or electric locomotives. In the case of roads, maintenance is supposed to keep them more or less in their original condition and costs do not rise significantly with age; modernization is, therefore, dictated essentially by obsolescence considerations such as large increases in traffic volume beyond road capacity, the use of heavier or bigger trucks, and higher speeds or changes in the location of industries. Port facilities might become obsolescent because of the use of larger ships or a shift to container shipments of general cargo.

Once the investments needed to increase capacity, to replace old equipment and to modernize have been identified, the next step is to determine priorities among them. This involves generalized cost-benefit comparisons which are refined at a later stage, when feasibility studies of individual projects are undertaken. At the level of the transport sector program, for example, it is not possible to make detailed forecasts for each individual road section, and forecasts must, therefore, be limited to such broad categories as short- and long-distance freight and passenger traffic, by major types of road. Similarly, it is sufficient to use general criteria for unit benefits, such as the reduction in vehicle operating costs when gravel roads are paved, or the value of the time of ships when port congestion is reduced. For railways, it is sufficient to focus on the half dozen major commodities and to use more generalized assumptions for estimating general cargo traffic. Since the purpose of a sector program is to avoid major misinvestments—not all

28

mistakes—the degree of refinement depends essentially on the probability of error from generalizations.

Priorities should be determined not only for each transport mode, but also among modes; most transport programs are deficient in this respect. There are two special problems in establishing priorities. First, as indicated above, comparisons are difficult when the quality of service varies widely as it does between rail and road. Secondly, while techniques for calculating the benefits of cost-reducing investments are reasonably satisfactory, the benefits of capacity expansion to handle more traffic are difficult to calculate because they involve estimating the net value of the additional output. In feasibility studies, such estimates are essential but there are few valid general criteria available for ready application in preparing a sector program.

Determining the proper over-all size of the transport program requires, in principle, a comparison of the marginal transport investments with those in other sectors, such as education, agriculture or even defense. Economics at this stage has not developed adequate tools for such intersector comparisons. In theory, all transport investments are justified with a rate of return higher than the country's opportunity cost of capital, but in practice programs based on this criterion have generally been larger than seemed justified for other reasons. There may be a number of reasons for this, such as the failure to use proper shadow rates for capital, labor and foreign exchange, the chronic underestimation of costs, institutional rigidities which prevent the free flow of funds into transport or a particular mode, or the failure to work out project interrelationships, with resultant over-capacity. There are, also, technical limitations in that many highway departments, for example, are inadequately staffed for the efficient planning and execution of road works, so that sharp increases in investments cannot be undertaken quickly. This is much less the case for railways, which tend to be better organized.

The transport program should indicate not only the physical investments needed, their costs, priority and timing, but also how the program should be financed. There are essentially three major sources of finance: charges on the users of transport services (whether earmarked or not), revenues from general taxation and domestic borrowing, and foreign aid. The first requires, for example, a forecast of railway revenues and expenditures to indicate to what extent the railway will be able to finance its investments from depreciation reserves and profits; if such internal sources are inadequate to finance a reasonable share of new investments, it may be appropriate to increase tariffs. Similarly, the level of road user charges or port charges will have to be examined to determine possible financing from these sources. The foreign exchange costs of the investment program need to be determined because foreign lending is frequently restricted to the financing of imports—foreign costs, by the way, must also be known because the official foreign exchange rate may not properly reflect the scarcity value of foreign exchange, and in order to determine the possibilities for import substitution. While the amount of foreign assistance is only to a limited extent within the control of developing countries, the distribution of investment financing between the budget and transport users is, and in most countries a much greater emphasis can and should be placed on financing through adequate user charges.

The preparation of transport programs will in the future be assisted by several transport models currently being built and tested, such as the one constructed at Harvard University with the assistance of the Brookings Institution. Harvard has developed two basic models. A macro-economic model furnishes basic regional production and consumption data which are used as input to the transport model; the latter in turn provides transport costs and distribution patterns for the macro-economic model. In this way it is possible to show the impact of changes in the economy on the transport sector and vice versa. Transport models are designed to describe how the producers of commodities would use a given transport network to reach what they consider to be desirable markets. These models attempt to express in mathematical form the many interrelationships between costs, traffic flows and outputs; they could, for example, show the costs of moving traffic by different routes or modes, including not only the direct transport costs but also the "costs" of time, damage, irregularity of delivery, etc. When there are many alternatives which must be considered, use of an electronic computer is essential.

None of the available models has yet been fully tested and it is quite clear that they must be used with caution. For example, the basic data must be sound; mere reliance on existing relationships is insufficient if these are distorted by government policies or inefficient operations. The analysis must be handled by experienced transport experts to avoid nonsense solutions, such as the shipping of bananas by pipeline. There can, however, be no doubt that models will become an increasingly important tool in transport planning.

CONCLUSION

The preparation of a transport sector program can be a useful effort but is not necessarily so. On the one hand, the costs are relatively small. A review of a dozen recent transport surveys indicates that the costs of preparing a ten-year program are generally less than one-fifth of one per cent of the investments. This is not an adequate criterion because a major purpose of transport planning is to minimize the need for new investments. Nevertheless, it indicates that if at least $200,000 can be saved in an investment program of $100 million, the survey is already justified. Experience indicates that the potential benefits are usually much larger than costs of this magnitude. On the other hand, there is probably little merit in preparing a transport program if it is merely to be a one-time effort because the government is not fully dedicated to economic development, or if the government is unable to carry out the difficult policies and measures needed for an efficient, well-coordinated transportation system.

II

ECONOMIC EVALUATION OF
TRANSPORT PROJECTS*

INTRODUCTION

Background

The economic art of evaluating transport projects in less developed countries is still primitive, but whether the discrepancy between theory and application is greater than in medicine, for example, is difficult to judge. This article describes the generally prevailing status of the art among those who have had perhaps the greatest experience with it, discusses some of the major problems, and makes a number of suggestions for further improvements. The main emphasis is on the evaluation of highways because they usually present greater difficulties for economic evaluation and because in the future their expansion is likely to be more important in most developing countries than that of other modes of transport. However, the methods and techniques discussed are of general applicability.

---

* This article is essentially the same as the one previously published in *Transport Investment and Economic Development,* edited by Gary Fromm, The Brookings Institution, 1965.

The economic evaluation of public works projects has been developed most extensively in connection with water-resource measures, such as flood control, navigation and soil conservation. It received its initial impetus in the United States in the 1930's when legislation required the Bureau of Reclamation, the Army Corps of Engineers and other agencies to measure costs and benefits and to use such measurements in the selection of particular projects. There have been many of these studies in the last ten years, with particular emphasis on water resources.

In the transportation field, the evaluation of railway projects and to some extent also of shipping and port projects, was usually limited to a financial analysis to determine whether future revenues could cover costs. In recent years a few railroads have adopted more formal capital budgeting methods. Economic evaluations, however, became a necessity with highways since they do not generally produce direct revenues. In the United States, the first ones were made by engineers in state highway departments in the late 1930's. Their use in less developed countries did not become extensive until a few years ago under the impetus of various foreign aid programs.

There is, of course, no causal relation between the backwardness of the economics of transport evaluation and the fact that until a few years ago it was virtually the exclusive domain of engineers. On the contrary, this condition is to a considerable extent due to the failure of economists to interest themselves in this area even though it is one in which close cooperation between economists and engineers is especially important. As a result, some of the most common mistakes in project evaluation result from the failure to apply economic criteria correctly or at all. A few of these mistakes, such as the failure to distinguish between private and public costs and benefits and between average and marginal costs, are discussed below.

A very special problem in less developed countries is the absence of basic statistics; this is frequently decisive for the degree of accuracy and refinement possible in the analysis. Most of these countries have, for example, initiated only very recently the collection of highway traffic data. Where statistics are available, they are usually limited to simple traffic counts; information on origin and destination of traffic or on the types of commodities carried on highways is hardly ever available. Little is usually known about vehicle operating costs on different types of highway or about road maintenance expenditures on different types of surface. As a result, most new investments and the allocation of maintenance expenditures have usually been made virtually without any detailed economic analyses of priorities. It is no doubt true that, within limits, some of the most obvious investments can be made simply by looking at a map and at the location of major industries and population centers. But this is not true after the most obvious highways have been constructed, nor does such a simple approach permit an adequate judgment about priorities over time, among the modes of transport, or between transport and investments in other fields. The absence of basic statistics, however, is not only a cause of the backward status of much analysis in this field but also an effect; because until recently economists have not focused on the right questions, there has been little incentive for collecting the right statistics.

Preliminary Steps

Before a specific transport project can be properly evaluated, two preliminary steps are highly desirable and usually essential in order gradually to reduce the consideration of alternatives to the project. The first step consists of a general economic survey of the country. Such a survey has two major functions. The first is to establish the country's over-all transportation needs by exploring, for example, the rate of economic growth and the resultant expansion in traffic. The second is to provide a basis for appraising the transport needs against the requirements of other sectors of the economy. This is not something that can be done very precisely, and it depends heavily on qualitative judgments. It is interesting that several such surveys have suggested that too much was being spent on transport investments. A recent survey of Colombia, for example, found that investments in education, housing and health deserved greater priority than marginal investments in trans-

35

port. Such surveys are also needed to help decide whether by changes in the location of industries, the total demand for transport can be reduced, and at what cost. The failure to make such surveys has led to transport investments, as well as recommendations for additional investments in some countries, which are out of line with the total investment resources of the country and with the priorities of other sectors.

The second step, which is the subject of the first article, should be a detailed transportation survey of the country in order to determine the priorities within that sector. Examples of this are transportation surveys made in recent years in Argentina, Brazil, Colombia, Ecuador, Korea, Nepal and Taiwan under World Bank auspices. Such surveys, if they are to be of maximum usefulness, should not only establish the broad framework of priorities for each mode of transport, such as the listing of highways in order of their importance, but should also indicate the proper role for each mode and the priorities among them. Such a transport program will be subject to later revision when specific projects are analyzed in detail. Unless both a general economic and a transportation survey precede the evaluation of a specific project, there is a considerable risk that the evaluation may be sufficiently incomplete as to lead to a misallocation of resources.

PROBLEMS OF PROJECT EVALUATION

The basic purpose of the economic evaluation of a project is to measure its economic costs and benefits in order to determine whether its net benefits are at least as great as those obtainable from other marginal investment opportunities in the particular country. There are, of course, many costs and benefits other than economic ones, such as the cultural opportunities from greater travel and the military and administrative advantages, and sometimes disadvantages, from greater mobility. These are not considered here because they have been excluded by definition, and also because, for better or for worse, they are not a main consideration for lending by most sources of foreign finance, whose primary purpose is to stimulate economic development. Nevertheless, these other benefits and costs are quite real and should be taken into account by the country involved.

It is sometimes stated that the value of a project should be measured by its contribution to the growth of national income as conventionally measured. This is not inconsistent with the above formulation, but it is not a practical approach. For one, it would exclude certain benefits altogether, such as greater comfort from an improved highway, or the time-saving used for more leisure, which would not be reflected in national income. More important, the national income approach is too complicated and indirect and in underdeveloped countries is simply not feasible. For example, if transport costs are reduced, an analysis would have to be made on how the freed resources are used in the future in other sectors of the economy to determine the resultant increase in national income. However, the national income approach is useful in focusing on costs and benefits from the point of view of the economy as a whole and not merely of the parties directly involved. In this way it helps in selecting the benefits to be included and those to be omitted and in avoiding counting the same benefit twice in different forms, such as when an improved highway reduces transport costs and increases land values. It is helpful in identifying economic costs and benefits, but not in measuring them.

In evaluating a project which consists of a number of separable and independent subprojects, separate economic analyses should be made of each subproject. Otherwise it is quite possible that the extra large benefits of one subproject may hide the insufficient benefits of another. For example, in the case of a port expansion project in Central America, the engineers recommended the construction of two new wharves. The economic justification indicated an economic rate of return on the investment of about 12 per cent, which was a satisfactory rate in the particular country. However, when separate analyses were made for each wharf, it turned out that the rate of return on one was nearly 20 per cent, while that on the other was only about 4 per cent even after allowance was made for the extra costs of building it separately; the second wharf was clearly not justified. The same principle applies especially to various

37

degrees of highway improvements and frequently also to different highway sections.

In order to measure economic benefits and costs and to compare them with other investment opportunities, they must be expressed in monetary terms, which are the only practical common denominator. This presents a problem since market prices do not reflect real costs to the extent that workable competition does not prevail in major sectors of the economy. In addition to any generally applicable limitations on competition in less developed countries, there are two special problems in the transport field. The first one arises from the fact that some transportation services by their very nature are oligopolistic or even monopolistic, so that the prices charged for these services frequently have no direct relation to costs. The most obvious example is the historic pricing of railway services whereby freight rates for particular commodities are not based on the costs of transporting these commodities but on the value of the commodity. A second related problem arises from the direct and indirect subsidization of many transportation services by governments. A generally applicable example is the provision of highways. In most developing countries gasoline taxes and other charges on the beneficiaries do not cover the costs of highways (including capital costs, maintenance and administration); even where they may cover over-all costs, there is usually no direct relation between specific user charges and the differing costs of the various transport services, such as those of trucks, buses and passenger cars.

These difficulties can be met, if not completely eliminated, by the use of "shadow prices" to reflect real economic costs and benefits more closely.

MEASURING ECONOMIC COSTS

The Use of Shadow Prices

Measuring the economic costs of a project is substantially simpler than measuring its economic benefits and can usually be limited to making adjustments in the actual expenses to the extent that they do not adequately reflect real economic costs. Three classes of costs for which such adjustments are usually necessary, i.e. for which "shadow prices" must be determined, are discussed below.

The first example is sales and other indirect taxes. The tax on gasoline, for instance, is a cost to those who pay the tax, but it does not necessarily reflect economic costs to the country as a whole in the sense that an increase in the tax does not mean that more economic resources are required to produce a given volume of gasoline. It is interesting that the famous report *Road User Bene-fit Analyses for Highway Improvements* by the American Association of State Highway Officials erroneously includes taxes in its measurement of fuel costs and thus fails to distinguish between private and public costs (and benefits). Similarly, license fees and import duties should be excluded, and adjustments should be made for the costs of imports at artificial exchange rates.

A second example is wages. In most countries minimum wage laws and other regulations and inflexibilities have the result that some wages actually paid do not correctly measure the real or opportunity costs of labor. Where an economy is marked by extensive unemployment or underemployment, the real costs of the type of labor involved are much less than actual wage rates. When this is a widely prevailing condition and is likely to remain so for some time, as in many less developed countries, the cost of labor, especially unskilled labor, should be calculated at substantially less than actual wage payments. On the other hand, it would also appear that the real costs of skilled labor may be greater than the wages paid. The same considerations are also applicable on the benefit side. In measuring the benefits of labor-saving equipment, the real benefit is substantially less if the replaced labor remains unemployed for a significant period during the economic life of the equipment.

A final example concerns interest. Interest actually paid is the financial cost of capital, which frequently has no relation to its economic cost, i.e. the opportunity cost of capital. Investment funds provided by governments for transportation are often made available at rates below the cost to the government; even if they cover the government's costs, the latter do not reflect economic costs if the funds were obtained by the government under direct or indirect compulsion, such as by taxation or by requiring banks to lend to the government below market rates. Funds obtained from foreign sources very frequently carry interest rates substantially below the opportunity cost of capital in less developed countries.

The economic cost of capital is very difficult to determine in the absence of free markets, especially since prevailing interest rates also reflect such factors as inflation and risk. The World Bank has made a number of studies attempting to measure the opportunity cost of capital in selected countries. While they do not permit any definitive judgments, they do indicate a range from about 6 to 12 per cent for the particular countries selected, and there is reason to believe that in most developing countries the rate is at least 8 per cent and frequently more than 10 per cent. Whether market interest rates or a lower (or perhaps higher) social rate should be used in discounting costs and benefits is beyond the scope of this article. As a practical matter, however, investments in less developed countries which show rates of return below 8 per cent deserve very special scrutiny.

The problem of the appropriate interest rate can be minimized somewhat in the evaluation of many projects by expressing the results in terms of an internal rate of return on the investment, rather than in terms of benefit-cost ratio. This is discussed further in the final section below.

Other Types of Adjustment

In addition to the use of shadow prices, there are other types of adjustment which are frequently necessary for an economic evaluation. The three examples given below are selected primarily because they illustrate mistakes which occur frequently.

In calculating the costs of a project, engineers usually include a contingency for unforeseen expenses. These are of two types.

First, costs may be greater than anticipated because the work turns out to be more difficult or more extensive; for example, more earth may have to be moved or the soil conditions may be less favorable than indicated by the sample data on which the cost estimate was based. In another case, costs may be greater because generally prevailing inflationary conditions increase wages and prices. For the purpose of economic analysis, this second element of the contingency allowance should not be included under costs, nor should a general inflation in the prices of benefits be taken into account. However, changes in relative prices should be allowed for to the extent that they are foreseeable and are likely to affect costs and benefits differently.

A second common error involves the treatment of interest during the construction period. Such interest is usually included in the costs of those projects which are financed by loans, such as new equipment for a railroad or the construction of a toll road, but it is frequently excluded where the project is financed by grants from general revenues, as in the case of most highways. This important financial distinction has no significance as far as the economic costs of the project are concerned since the real resources used—labor, material, equipment, etc.—are the same regardless of the source of financing. Money is the means of procuring these real economic resources, so that interest should not be included in the economic costs of the project.

However, interest is relevant in a quite different sense. Since the benefits of a project do not begin until some time after the project has been started and costs have been incurred, it becomes necessary to compare costs and benefits beginning in different years and having different time streams. Regardless of the financing method, the timing of costs is an important element since a cost incurred this year has a different economic value than the same cost incurred some time in the future. To measure the difference, future costs can be expressed in terms of present values by discounting them at an appropriate interest rate. The proper method of comparing benefits and costs with different time streams is, therefore, to discount all future costs and benefits as of the time a cost is first in-

41

curred. Under this method, interest (as well as depreciation) is implicitly allowed for, so that adding interest to the costs would involve double counting.

An alternative method which is sometimes used includes interest during construction and discounts benefits as of the first year they begin, which is generally some time after the first costs are incurred. This tends to confuse the financial with the economic analysis since usually the interest included in costs is the interest actually paid. In most cases, this has no direct relation either to the opportunity cost of capital or to the internal rate of return by which the benefits should be discounted, so that, in effect, the costs are discounted by a rate different from that used for benefits. It should also be noted that this method actually overstates costs where benefits begin before the project is completed, which occurs quite frequently in highway construction. There seems to be no particular advantage in discounting costs and benefits to a year other than the year in which the project starts, which is nearly always the first year in which costs are incurred.

A third mistake, which only deserves mention because it occurs quite often, arises from the failure to define properly the scope of the project with the result that project costs do not include all relevant costs. For example, a toll road authority in a developing country included in the costs of a new road only the expenses for which it would be responsible. This, however, failed to take into account the necessity for improving access roads. Since the improvement of access roads was essential for the effective utilization of the toll road, the costs involved should have been included in the project costs for the purpose of economic evaluation, even though they could properly be excluded for an analysis of the authority's financial position. In this particular instance it was probable that the access roads would have been improved in time in any case. Therefore, it became necessary to establish the additional costs of making the improvements earlier than would otherwise have been the case and of the higher design standards needed for the greater volume of traffic caused by the toll road.

MEASURING ECONOMIC BENEFITS

Introduction

Measuring the economic benefits of transport projects is usually much more difficult than measuring their economic costs. There are a number of reasons for this. First, some benefits, even though quite direct—such as the increased comfort and convenience from an improved road—are difficult to express in monetary terms since there are usually no market prices for such benefits. Second, monetary benefits, such as reduced transport costs, affect a great number of people over a long period of time, requiring difficult long-range forecasts. Third, many benefits are indirect, such as the stimulation to the economy from improved transportation; for these benefits to materialize, investments in fields other than transport are frequently necessary.

The most important benefits from transport projects include: (1) reduced operating expenses initially to the users of the new facility and also usually to those who continue to use the existing facilities; (2) lower maintenance costs; (3) fewer accidents and less damage to goods; (4) savings in time for both passengers and freight; (5) increased comfort, convenience and reliability; and (6) stimulation of economic development. Not all of these benefits result from all projects, and their respective importance differs from project to project. At the present state of the art of project evaluation, those listed near the beginning can frequently be measured in monetary terms more easily than the others. This article will not deal with the measurement of maintenance costs and of comfort and convenience. The former offers probably the least difficult conceptual problems, and the latter would seem to have a relatively low social value in developing countries, even though to judge by differences between first- and second-class railway service, it has a considerable private value.

Before discussing the problems of measuring the remaining benefits, it may be useful to refer to a matter which is rarely considered in their evaluation, i.e. the distribution of benefits among the beneficiaries. For example, if the improvement of a port reduces the turn-around time of ships, much of the benefit might go initially to foreign ship owners; the degree to which they pass it on to the country paying for the investment depends largely on the degree of competition in shipping. Similarly, the improvement of a scenic highway may initially benefit foreign tourists primarily or those from other areas of the country. A government could, of course, adopt a policy of recouping some or most of these benefits by appropriate user charges. The matter of the distribution of benefits is therefore important in the selection of a policy of user charges which will channel the benefits to the desired recipients.

Perhaps even more important is the fact that the distribution of benefits affects their over-all size. For example, if a railway maintains previously existing freight rates even though a transport improvement has lowered costs, the consumers would not benefit directly, but the railway might have higher profits. A determination of the net benefits to the economy would depend on weighing what the railway would do with its higher profits (or the government with its "savings" from reduced losses) against the benefits from lower freight rates. An important consideration is that if the rates are not lowered, the transport improvement will hardly stimulate new traffic. Where there is reason to believe that the likely distribution of benefits either reduces their over-all size or is inconsistent with other public policies, the problem deserves greater attention than it now usually receives, with special emphasis on appropriate user charges.

Reduced Operating Expenses

The most direct benefit from a new or improved transport facility, and frequently also the most important and the one most readily measurable in monetary terms, is the reduction of transport costs (see Paper No. 2 in the World Bank series). While this benefit accrues initially to the users of the facility, competition or the desire to maximize profits leads them to share it in various degrees with other groups, such as producers, shippers and consumers. The

44

cost reduction therefore benefits the nation as a whole and not merely the users of the facility.

The first step in measuring the benefit from reduced costs is to estimate the future use of the facility, i.e. the future traffic during its useful life. The useful life of a facility is limited primarily by economic change and technical obsolescence, caused by, for example, changes in markets and new or improved processes. These are much less predictable than the facility's physical life. While forecasts of service life are therefore to some extent inevitably speculative, the discounting of far-off periods makes these relatively unimportant. In many cases, for example, it will make little difference whether the life of a highway is taken as twenty-five or thirty years.

Future traffic can be broken down into three main types: the "normal", the "diverted" and the "generated" traffic. The "normal" traffic growth is that which would have taken place on the existing facilities, even without the new investment. This type of traffic benefits by the full reduction in operating costs made possible by the new facility, since, by definition, this traffic would otherwise have traveled even at the higher (and perhaps steadily increasing) costs of the existing facility.

The proper standard for measuring the savings in vehicle operating costs is provided by the "with and without" test: what will the costs be with the new facility and what would they have been without it? In numerous project evaluations, however, a quite different standard is mistakenly applied—the "before and after" test: what were the costs before the new facility was constructed and what will they be afterwards? As shown below, this test usually leads to a serious underestimate of economic benefits.

For example, in connection with the evaluation of a new expressway in Japan, the responsible authorities measured the operating costs of a truck on the existing highway in 1958; they were about US 15 cents equivalent per kilometer, excluding taxes. The costs on the new expressway, which is scheduled to be opened in 1969, were estimated at 11 cents, or a saving of 4 cents per truck/kilo-meter. This saving was then applied to the estimated truck traffic for the years 1969 to 1979; no increase in traffic was assumed thereafter because the so-called design capacity of the expressway would then be reached and vehicle operating costs would there-after begin to increase. This approach, which is based on the "before and after" test, illustrates a number of common mistakes. The first is that the comparison of costs on the existing highway in 1958 with those on the new expressway in 1969 fails to take into account the important fact that the increasing congestion on the existing highway would have increased operating expenses con-siderably by 1969 over those prevailing in 1958. Secondly, the operating costs on the existing highway would have continued to increase after 1969, while those on the new expressway are likely to remain relatively stable for ten years and the increase thereafter is likely to be less sharp than on the existing highway. The situa-tion is illustrated by the figure below.

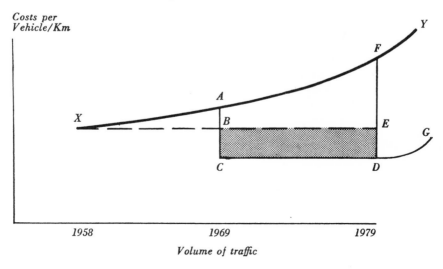

Here, XY represents the truck operating costs on the existing highway, assuming the expressway is not built. It slopes upward in time because of increasing congestion. By the time the express-way is opened in 1969, the costs have already increased somewhat over the 1958 level. The reduction in operating costs per truck, according to the "before and after" test, is BC throughout the life of the new investment, and the benefits (through 1979) are represented by the shaded area of BCDE. Actually, the reduction is AC when the facility is opened in 1969, DF by 1979, and the benefits are at least ACDF. Also, it is questionable whether no increase in traffic should be assumed after 1979. The concept of highway capacity is hardly a scientific one and the traffic on the existing highway is more than double the design capacity. The real issue is at what point new investment is justified in order to increase capacity further. Determining the optimum timing involves weighing the benefits of reduced congestion against the costs of undertaking the investment rather than postponing it a year. Depending on the lumpiness of the investment, traffic increases substantially beyond design capacity may be justified before expanding the capacity further.

It is sometimes stated that when the increasing costs of growing congestion, i.e. the difference between the CG and the AY curves, are properly taken into account, the growth in vehicle operating savings tends to be twice as great as the growth in traffic. While such generalizations have to be treated carefully, a few actual cases indicate that it may sometimes serve as a rough approximation. For example, a study of a road improvement in Jamaica indicated that it would reduce operating costs by about £40,000 in 1963. If this benefit is increased by the estimated annual traffic growth of 12 per cent, it would reach £70,000 in 1968 and £120,-000 in 1973. If, however, the increasing costs of further congestion are allowed for, the benefit would be £90,000 in 1968 and £250,000 in 1973. The difference would become even greater in the following years.

The application of the erroneous "before and after" test can lead to curious results. In connection with a proposed highway improvement in Syria, investigation showed vehicle operating costs on the existing highway to be quite reasonable; it had a fair surface and a satisfactory width. Unfortunately, the highway was not constructed to carry the prevailing heavy loads, and engineers advised that it would break up in about two years and that, even

47

with heavy maintenance expenditures, a complete reconstruction would be necessary. However, vehicle operating costs would not be significantly lower thereafter. The "before and after" test indicated that the reconstruction would bring only modest benefits and would not be justified, at least not at that time. The "with and without" test, however, indicated that without the new investment, vehicle operating costs would go up very sharply, to say nothing of maintenance costs; the avoidance of this increase should in this case have been the proper basis for the economic evaluation of the benefits.

The above examples have been limited to highways, but the analysis is in principle identical for railways or ports. For example, in 1963 the Spanish Railway developed a ten-year modernization and expansion program estimated to cost about US $1 billion equivalent. In addition to evaluating the benefits from individual components of the program, it was also desired to measure the return on the program as a whole. Analysis showed that the program would reduce operating costs by about 25 per cent between 1963 and 1973. When this benefit was measured against the investment costs of the modernization part of the program, it showed an internal rate of return of about 15 per cent. This "before and after" approach, however, understated the benefits significantly since in the absence of the new investments, operating costs would not have remained at the 1963 level, but would have increased. When allowance was made for this, the rate of return on the investment became about 18 per cent.

The second type of traffic is that which is diverted to the new facility either from other modes of transport or from other routes. The benefit for diverted traffic is measured by the difference in transport costs on the old route or mode of transport and on the new facility. There are, however, two special problems which should be kept in mind in measuring this benefit. The first is that the relevant costs in this connection are not the average costs of transport on both facilities, but the avoidable costs, i.e. the amounts that would be saved. If, for example, traffic is diverted from a railway to a new highway, the benefits cannot be measured by comparing the transport costs on the new road with either

48

railway charges or even average railway costs, but by comparing them with the marginal costs of carrying the diverted traffic by railway. If the diverted traffic is only a small part of the railway's total traffic and if the railway has excess capacity, the marginal savings would be substantially less than indicated by a comparison of average costs; this is probably the usual case. While the available data in most developing countries do not permit precise estimates of marginal costs, the understanding of the correct concepts is essential for making the best use of the data which are available.

Comparing costs of different transport modes presents a further practical problem in that the transport services provided by each mode usually differ substantially and must therefore be reduced to a common denominator. Total distribution costs are the primary concern, not just the cost of shipment. For example, comparing the cost of coastal shipping traffic diverted to a highway must take into account not merely shipping costs, but also such additional costs as loading and unloading, storage, insurance, breakage, delays, etc. These additional costs may readily add 50 per cent to the basic shipping costs. Similarly, in comparing the costs of railway and highway transport, adequate allowance must be made for the fact that trucking is a door-to-door service, while railway service will generally require two loadings and unloadings, which, in addition to the direct costs, frequently involve delays and breakage.

Another type of diverted traffic consists of a change from one type of conveyance to another on the same route, such as passenger trips previously made by bus but now made by private car. In this case, the higher relative operating costs of a private car are evidently outweighed by its qualitative advantages, especially the greater convenience and comfort. It is usually not possible to measure this difference in monetary terms.

While the benefits to the economy are measured by the reduction of social costs (costs excluding taxes for instance), it is not the social but the private costs which are relevant in estimating the amount of traffic diversion. In fact, since many people make decisions on driving largely on the basis of out-of-pocket costs, it is the difference between these and railway rates actually charged (regardless of cost) which will largely decide the amount of passenger traffic which will be diverted from a railway to a highway.

The third type of traffic is that which is newly generated as a result of the lowering of transport costs and which previously did not exist at all. This includes traffic both from increases in industrial or agricultural production caused by the cheaper transport as well as transport not associated with an increase in production, such as the transport of commodities previously sold locally but now transported to markets where a better price can be obtained.

As far as reductions in transport costs are concerned, it would not be appropriate to apply the total reduction in unit operating costs to this traffic since it would not have materalized without the reduction. If there is reason to believe that in a particular situation the traffic would have been generated with a transport cost reduction of only a quarter the actual reduction, it would be appropriate to apply three-quarters of the unit cost reduction to the generated traffic. In the many situations where the available data do not permit a judgment on the relationship between the degree of transport cost reduction and the volume of generated traffic, perhaps the most reasonable assumption is that this traffic would have developed in proportion to the reduction in transport costs; if so, it would be appropriate to apply approximately one-half of the unit cost reductions to this traffic.

To the extent that the main purpose of a new transport facility is to open up new lands for cultivation or to otherwise make possible new economic development, reductions in transport costs for generated traffic are not a useful measure of the economic benefits of the project. In this situation, the benefit consists of the new production made possible; the problems of measuring this benefit are discussed later.

Accident Reduction

Accident reduction is clearly an economic benefit, but not every transport improvement reduces accidents; whether it does or not must be investigated in each case. For example, it is quite possible that an improved highway may initially increase not only the number of accidents, but, more importantly, the accident rate per vehicle/km and the severity of each accident. This could happen where the increased speed is not offset by additional safety factors, especially in a country where automobile driving is still in its initial stages and the discipline required for safe driving is equally underdeveloped. Accident reduction is apparently most significant for expressways with divided lanes and controlled access.

Measuring the economic benefits involves two main steps. The first is to estimate the reduction in accidents, which entails, for example, comparing the accident rate on the existing highway as it would be in the absence of the improvement, with the rate on higher standard highways within the country or, if necessary, in other countries (but making allowance for national differences).

The second step is to estimate the value of the accident reduction. For this purpose, it is useful to consider three types of damages. The one most readily measurable in monetary terms is property damage, usually to the cars involved in the accident. Police statistics in Japan, for example, indicate that the average property damage per accident is about US $600 equivalent. This may not be an unreasonable figure—though it should be adjusted for excise taxes, among other things—since about two-thirds of the traffic is accounted for by trucks and buses, with a relatively low average age. Reduced breakage of cargo can also be a significant benefit. The cost of injuries is more difficult to measure. In the Japanese studies this was estimated at about US $100 equivalent per accident, which includes an allowance both for loss of earnings and for the cost of medical treatment for the injured who were over fourteen years of age.

Finally, to measure fatality reduction, there is the problem of putting a value on life. In the Japanese case, this was calculated by capitalizing the average annual income per worker over a thirty-year period. This is obviously a highly controversial proposition. At a minimum there should be deducted from gross income the future resources needed to produce that income. It would be too callous to suggest that if a country is overpopulated, the social and the private values of the fatality reduction would be quite different. On balance, it would seem preferable not to express fatality reduction in monetary terms. In any case accident reduction in the less developed countries is likely to be of minor significance compared to other benefits, and the reduction of fatalities is only a small part of accident reduction. Fatalities can either be neglected in most cases or simply expressed in terms of the number of deaths involved. An exception to this conclusion would be investments whose very purpose is to reduce accidents, such as safety measures in the aviation field; it then becomes quite essential to express fatality reduction in monetary terms.

Time Savings

Even though most transport improvements reduce travel time, the value of time for passengers and freight is frequently omitted from project evaluations. This may lead to a serious underestimate of benefits since time savings can be substantial. Related to this is the benefit from greater reliability of transport services.

As far as persons are concerned, time can be money, but it need not be. Whether it is depends primarily on how the opportunities made possible by the increased availability of time are used—whether for increased production or voluntary leisure, on the one hand, or for involuntary idleness, on the other. Unfortunately, in many developing countries there is extensive underemployment, so that time savings may merely make the situation worse. But even here, time savings for entrepreneurs, for example, may be very valuable.

What can be done to measure the value of time may be illustrated by a recent study in Japan, where a new expressway was to reduce travel time very substantially. All travelers were divided into two classes: the relatively few who can afford to travel in private cars, and the many who travel in buses. As a first step, the average value of time was related to the per capita income of the two classes. This showed that in one hour, travelers in cars could earn at least US $1 equivalent, while those in buses at least US 20 cents. Since there are ample employment opportunities in Japan, this calculation was not unreasonable.

However, to check on its validity, these average values were compared with the amounts people are actually willing to pay for time. For this purpose, a study was made of surcharges imposed by the railway for different types of trains running between the same cities. On the Tokaido line, for example, travelers have an ample choice between different trains, ranging from slow, local trains to very fast expresses. While between some of these trains speed is not the only difference, convenience and comfort being others, it is the most important one and between at least two of them it is probably the only difference. An analysis of these surcharges indicates that travelers are willing to pay at least US $2 equivalent in first class and US $1 equivalent in second per hour saved. These findings and those based on the earnings method give a clear indication of the range of values that might be given to time savings of passengers. They suggest that in Japan, at least, many individuals prefer to take these time savings in the form of leisure even if they could devote them to income-producing activities. This is probably not true in most underdeveloped countries. In any case, since the time savings will presumably exist for the life of the project, allowance should be made for the increasing value of time as per capita income grows. (Time savings for truck and bus drivers are generally allowed for under calculations of vehicle operating savings.)

Time saved on the shipment of freight may well be more valuable in the less developed countries than in those more advanced. Freight tied up during transit is in fact capital, and is therefore of particular importance where capital is in short supply. This saving can be measured by the price of capital; i.e. the rate of interest. In addition, faster delivery, which is usually accompanied by more reliable delivery, reduces spoilage and makes possible lower inventories, which in turn is an additional form of capital saving. Beyond this, where larger inventories are not possible, a delay may immobilize other resources, as where the absence of a spare part may prevent the utilization of expensive equipment.

As in the case of time savings for travelers, a study was made in Japan on the prices shippers are willing to pay for different types of transport services, where time is by far the major and in some cases perhaps the only difference. The study covered a dozen important commodities and indicated, for example, the following prices actually paid for a saving of one ton/hour (in US cents):

Dairy products	35
Fresh fish	21
Vegetables	20
Fruit	14
Minerals	1

The relative importance of time savings and other benefits depends of course on the nature of the particular project. That it can be very significant is indicated by the project for which the above studies were made. In this case, the value of time savings was nearly half as great as the benefits from lower vehicle operating costs.

Economic Development

It is frequently assumed that all transport improvements stimulate economic development. The sad truth is that some do, some do not, and that even some of those that do may not be economically justified in the sense that there may be better investment opportunities. Each project must therefore be investigated individually, and no helpful generalizations appear possible until more research shows that certain definite correlations do exist.

Before any transport improvement can be said to have stimulated economic development at all, a number of conditions must be met. The most important is showing that the economic development would not have taken place in any case without the transport improvement. A second is that the resources used in the new development would otherwise have remained unused or used less productively. Finally, it is essential that the economic activity stimulated does not replace equally productive activity which otherwise would have taken place.

These conditions may be obvious, but it is surprising how often they are forgotten in practice. In the sophisticated Japanese studies previously referred to, extensive research was undertaken to measure the growth in industrial output in the area of influence of a new highway, and there were strong reasons to believe that the highway and the output were indeed causally related. While this was very useful from a local point of view, it had much less significance for the economy as a whole. Further inquiry indicated that most of the resources used in the new production would not otherwise have remained unemployed and that the firms responsible for the new output had planned to expand in any case and picked a location near the new highway because of its advantages. From a national point of view, therefore, the highway cannot be regarded as having contributed significantly to stimulating new economic development. This is not to say that the locational shifts caused by the highway involved no economic benefits other than lower transport costs; they may have facilitated more efficient production, but this benefit can only have been a fraction of the total net output.

Where a transport facility does lead to increased output and the above conditions are met, the net value of this additional output is the proper measure of the economic benefit. (The net value of output and the vehicle operating savings for generated traffic are, of course, not additive.) In many situations, however, the transport facility is not the only new investment needed to achieve the increased production. This raises the problem of allocating the benefit, i.e. the increased production, among the transport and the other investments. For this there exists no correct theoretical answer and the proper approach is not to make an allocation at all, but to relate total benefits to total investments. An alternative presentation allocates the benefits in the same ratio as the transport investment to the other investments, but the result amounts essentially to the same as making no allocation. A third approach consists of annualizing the other investment costs and deducting them from the benefits. This is dangerous since it may lead to ascribing all the benefits arbitrarily to the transport investments; the error is likely to be small, however, if the non-transport investments are only a small part of the project.

Each of these solutions is appropriate in different situations. For example, in the actual case of new coal mining in Sarawak, it was necessary to build a road to transport the coal from the mine to a port. The estimates indicated that the coal would account for more than 90 per cent of the total traffic using the new road. The road was an integral part of the coal mining scheme—just as integral as the mining equipment—and had virtually no other use. In this case an allocation of benefits between the road and the investments in the mine would be meaningless. On the other hand, where a road is being built to facilitate new agricultural as well as industrial development—which will also require other major investments—an allocation of benefits might be more useful.

Where the transport facility enlarges the market for commodities previously produced, the economic benefit consists of the difference in value of the commodity in the old and the new market, minus the new costs of transport. For example, the price of a commodity in the old market may be 10 cents; in a second market it is 20 cents, but because transport costs are 12 cents, shipment to this market is uneconomic. Assuming a transport improvement that cuts transport costs in half, to 6 cents, the commodity can be delivered to the second market for 16 cents and there be sold for 20 cents. The benefit from the new investment (assuming resources before and after the change are fully employed) would be 4 cents. Account must be taken of the fact that the increased supply may affect prices in both markets; if so, the benefit is usually valued at prices prevailing after the transport improvement is completed. For passenger traffic, this benefit, i.e. the difference between staying at home and traveling, minus the transport costs, can usually not be measured in monetary terms.

What can be done in practice to measure the net value of increased production or of wider markets differs from case to case. For example, in the Sarawak illustration given above, detailed studies were made by various experts of the supply of coal, the costs of production and transport, and probable market prices. The problems are usually much more difficult for agricultural development because its success depends on the willingness and ability of a large number of people and the development potential of large areas. In the Sarawak case, the likely agricultural output attributable to the highway could be estimated within a satisfactory margin of error since only two commodities were involved and experience from previous transport improvements on land with a similar agricultural potential could serve as a reasonable guide for probable future output and the other investments needed to achieve it.

Where transport is intended to open up new land for development, three types of situation may usefully be distinguished. In the first, the transport facility is an integral part of an agricultural, industrial or mining project, such as the Sarawak illustration; in this case, the focus of the evaluation must be the entire project and on providing the least cost transport solution. The second situation is one where transport is clearly the only significant bottleneck to development and where all other requirements are already met. An example would be a road to connect an existing town and a nearby fruit-growing area, whose products are now being transported by animal or cart but where high transport costs alone prevent increased production. Finally, there is the frequent case where transport is built into a new area, which, though promising, will not develop unless other investments and improvements are also made. Transport investments in this last group are rarely justified unless accompanied by the other improvements.

The relationship between transport and development is an area where only very little research has so far been done. But it is clear that if the main purpose of a transport facility is to stimulate economic development, greater efforts must be made to measure this benefit—efforts similar to those now made for an irrigation scheme, for example. And if the economic development can be achieved only if the transport improvement is supplemented by other investments, extension service to farmers, land reform, etc., then these other measures become an essential condition of the project. This, too, has been recognized in the field of irrigation, but unfortunately not yet fully in transport.

COMPARING COSTS AND BENEFITS

Once costs and benefits have been measured in monetary terms to the full extent meaningful, the results can be put into at least three different forms: the internal rate of return on the investment, the benefit-cost ratio (or net present worth), and the pay-back period. A great deal has been written about these alternatives, so that the discussion here is limited to a few salient points.

There is unfortunately no uniformity in the application of these forms. In some benefit-cost ratios, for example, gross costs are compared with gross benefits, while in others, some costs are first deducted from the benefits; this can affect the ratio very substantially. Sometimes—and more correctly—it is the difference between benefits and costs which is used. In the case of rate of return calculations, the benefits are sometimes measured against the investment costs (with or without allowance for depreciation), or sometimes by the internal rate of return. It is essential to know exactly what formula is used if the final result is to be correctly interpreted.

While the basic ingredients—the value of the costs and benefits —are the same regardless of the final form in which they are expressed, the usefulness of the various forms is different, depending on the purpose. A short pay-back period is important where the future is unusually uncertain, where better investment opportunities are likely to arise soon, or where funds are not available on a long-term basis. These considerations are much more important for private businesses than for governments. Also, the fact that the benefits of an investment are large in the beginning may give no indication of what they are over the life of the investment, so that relative pay-back periods are a particularly poor method for comparing investments having a different time stream of benefits. Furthermore, there are superior techniques for incorporating uncertainty into investment analysis.

Discounting benefits and costs by the opportunity cost of capital is theoretically the best way of comparing different projects. Either the discounted costs can be subtracted from the discounted benefits to obtain the net present worth of the project, or the discounted benefits can be divided by discounted costs to obtain the benefit-cost ratio. If benefits of the project outweigh costs, net present worth is positive, and the benefit-cost ratio is larger than 1. The most important disadvantage of this approach is that a particular interest rate must be chosen for discounting. In practice, the interest rate mistakenly selected is frequently the one being paid, which may or may not have any relation to the opportunity cost of capital in the country. Unfortunately, the opportunity cost of capital is frequently not known or can be estimated only with a considerable margin of error. This is particularly crucial since the discount rate chosen is one of the major determinants of the benefit-cost comparison.

This disadvantage can be minimized somewhat by expressing benefits and costs in terms of the internal rate of return on the investment, i.e. the rate which equalizes discounted costs and benefits. In this case, the opportunity cost of capital becomes important only in the marginal cases where the internal rate of return is not clearly above or below the area within which the opportunity cost of capital may be estimated to be. For example, it would be virtually certain that an investment in Japan with a rate of return of 12 per cent is justified, since the opportunity cost of capital is less, probably between 6 and 10 per cent. But even where the two rates may be relatively close, the internal rate of return formula has the advantage of focusing directly on the crucial question: how the particular investment compares with the other investment opportunities. The benefit-cost ratio tends to hide this crucial point in assuming a certain interest rate.

On the other hand, the internal rate of return formula also has its disadvantages. While, as a practical matter, it usually leads to a correct choice of projects, it may sometimes be misleading in comparing projects having different lives and different time streams of benefits. In practice, however, transportation nearly always involves long-term investments and the time streams of benefits do not tend to vary drastically. Even where they do, the margin of error involved in an internal rate of return calculation may be less than discounting by the opportunity cost of capital, which is usually known only within a wide range. Also, where a project is compared not with a direct alternative but with investment opportunities in general, the internal rate is generally a perfectly satisfactory formula.

A theoretical disadvantage of the internal rate of return is that the answer may be ambiguous in that more than one rate may equalize costs and benefits. In practice this is rare in the case of transport projects, since the costs are predominantly incurred in the early stages and the benefits arise later, in which case the solution would be unique.

Finally, the rate of return formula has the practical advantage that economists, financial experts and many businessmen have some concept of what an interest rate is, so that a rate of return is probably more meaningful to many audiences than a benefit-cost ratio. On balance, the choice depends somewhat on one's position. The World Bank has found it satisfactory to use the internal rate of return in the evaluation of most projects which are submitted to it for financing. There are two major reasons for this: first, it has not been practical to estimate the opportunity cost of capital for the approximately eighty developing countries who are members of the Bank; second, the Bank must assure itself only that the project is justified, it need not be the highest priority project in the country. On the other hand, preparation of a development plan and the concomitant determination of relative priorities does require discounting by an opportunity cost of capital, so that this is the better method for countries planning their investments.

ANNEX

TERMS OF REFERENCE FOR A
TRANSPORT SURVEY

The terms of reference for a transport survey have to be tailored to the specific requirements of each country. While complete standardization is therefore not possible, terms of reference have to cover all or most of the subjects discussed in the text. The terms of reference for a reasonably typical survey are reproduced below; they are based on recent surveys in Bolivia, the Ivory Coast and Malaysia.

A review of half a dozen transport surveys indicates that the size of the effort, and therefore the staffing requirements and the cost, is related to such factors as the country's area and population, the stage of economic development, the size and diversification of the transport system, and the degree of detail required. Depending on these and other factors, foreign exchange costs for transport surveys ranging from $300,000 - 600,000 are not uncommon.

Requirements for a transport survey for Malaysia will illustrate staffing and costs more concretely. Malaysia has a population of nearly 10 million, a land area of 128,000 square miles, and a gross national product of about $3 billion (U.S. equivalent). Annual expenditures on transportation are approaching $250 million, of which about one-half is accounted for by private passenger cars. Two-thirds of total transport expenditures are in foreign exchange. During the 1966-70 Plan period, public investments in transport are estimated at $185 million.

Malaysia's road network totals over 11,000 miles, of which more than 80 per cent is paved; there are about a quarter of a million motor vehicles in the country, and about 180,000 motorcycles. The railway network connects most of the major towns and has about 1,000 miles of line; it has been carrying about 450 million ton/miles and 350 million passenger/miles annually in recent years. Malaysia has about six deep-water ports and twelve airports.

Malaysia consists of three separate regions far apart from each other, yet the country's transport problems are relatively less serious than those of many other developing countries. After a careful review of these problems, it was estimated that the survey would take about ten months.

While judgments on staffing may reasonably differ, one possible pattern of staffing by foreign experts was as follows: one project manager, three general, agricultural, or industrial economists, two transport economists, three highway experts, one highway transport expert, two railway experts, two port and shipping experts, and miscellaneous (e.g. aviation expert, etc.).

While at least the project manager, two of the five economists and one each of the modal experts would be full time on the assignment, most of the others would participate only part-time. The team would also receive support from staff in the consultants' home office. In addition, each of the foreign experts would have a Malaysian counterpart.

With this staffing pattern, the costs of the survey were estimated at about US $700,000 - 800,000; of this, about US $200,000 equivalent was in local currency, including the salaries of Malaysian counterparts and other staff. The survey started in mid-1967 and is estimated to be completed before mid-1968. Provision was also made for continuing advisory assistance in transport planning and for training Malaysians abroad.

The terms of reference for a transport survey follow.

I. OBJECTIVES

The purpose of this transport survey is to recommend improvements in the country's existing transport services and to formulate a coordinated development program for the transportation sector. To this end, the survey shall provide:

(a) a detailed program of transport investments for 1969-73, based on the economic priorities of specific projects;

(b) a perspective program of transport investments for 1974-83;

(c) recommendations for the improvement of the operation, planning, organization, administration and management of each transport mode;

(d) recommendations for the improvement of government transport policies, especially policies for effective transport coordination; and

(e) recommendations for the retention of advisors and the training abroad of the country's nationals in the field of transportation planning.

II. SCOPE OF CONSULTING SERVICES

A. General

This transport survey shall cover the entire country and all modes of transport that have a significant role in the country's national economy, including railways, highways and highway transport, ports and shipping, airports and civil aviation. The survey shall focus primarily on intercity traffic and will not include studies of intracity traffic, except to the extent that intercity traffic may be affected (e.g. bypasses and terminals in urban areas).

63

The consultants shall perform all technical and administrative studies, economic analyses, financial investigations, field investigations and related work herein described, as required to attain the objectives given in Section I hereof. In the conduct of this work, the consultants shall cooperate fully with the government which will provide data and services outlined in Section III hereof; however, the consultants shall be solely responsible for the analysis and interpretation of all data received and for the findings, conclusions and recommendations contained in their reports.

General policy guidance will be given to the consultants by a coordinating committee composed of representatives of the government and the International Bank for Reconstruction and Development.

B. Transport Studies

1. Review and Forecast of Transport Needs.

The consultants shall review and summarize all available data on passenger and freight traffic in foreign and domestic commerce, by all modes of transport, on the principal routes within the country. Breakdowns shall be prepared of traffic flows by mode and by principal commodities, indicating significant seasonal variations in flow. This review shall cover the transport history of the country for the past five years, but consideration shall also be given to transport data of earlier years, where such data may be of importance to future developments.

The government will advise the consultants of the policies of the government regarding the growth of national income, the development of various sectors of the economy and of the probable locations and sizes of future agricultural, industrial and mining developments and related storage facilities. The government will similarly advise the consultants on estimated future population and its location. The consultants shall review the information provided by the government on the prospective growth in each major sector of the economy and the expected volumes of production and consumption that may result therefrom.

Based on the identification and evaluation of all major traffic generating sources, the consultants shall prepare forecasts of the nature and volume of traffic flows which the country's transport system will have to accommodate in the years 1969 through 1975, and in more general terms between 1976 and 1985. In this connection, the consultants shall also advise on possible economies from alternative locations of new economic activity as far as transport is concerned.

2. *Analysis of Existing Transport System.*

(a) Railway. The consultants shall review all available data and reports on the existing railway system, make a general inspection of the network, and prepare an independent analysis of the physical, operational, organizational, administrative, economic and financial aspects of the system. This analysis shall take into account the present and anticipated future traffic demand related to mining, industrial, agricultural, and other developments in the regions served by the railway and the role of competitive modes of transport.

The consultants shall identify and analyze any practices relating to fiscal, staff, rating or other matters, which may operate against the railway being run efficiently and in a sound, commercial manner. In this connection, where present and estimated future traffic densities indicate that any section of an existing line is uneconomic, the consultants shall examine the availability and economic cost of possible alternative modes of transport.

Based on the foregoing, the consultants shall:
  (1) identify needed improvements in maintenance on the existing railway lines;
  (2) assess the need for extension, modification or phased abandonment of lines, where justified by expected traffic; and
  (3) define changes in operating methods, equipment, and practices that would result in more economical railway service.

(b) Highways and Highway Transport. The consultants shall review all available data and reports on the existing highway network. The consultants shall also conduct a visual inspection of all major and secondary roads and of approximately one-third of the tertiary roads. This inspection shall result in an inventory of the highway network that will indicate, by major road sections, the general geometric and construction standards (type of base, width and type of surfacing), capacity of structures, mileage, geographic distribution, present state of maintenance, and general adequacy for present traffic.

The consultants shall analyze all existing statistical data on highway traffic. If the consultants find that additional traffic counts and origin-destination studies are required to determine the nature of the traffic and the present volume of freight and passenger movements by road, the necessary additional counts and other field investigations will be undertaken by the appropriate government agency, under supervision of the consultants. The consultants shall also assist the agency in the establishment and operation of a continuous year-round traffic counting system over the primary and secondary roads which can serve to measure seasonal patterns and the yearly growth of traffic, in order to help determine the priority of future maintenance and improvement works on the entire system. In addition, the consultants shall review and comment on:

(1) the government's plans for future highway development;
(2) the present geometric and construction standards used by the government;
(3) the policies, organization, staffing, equipment, operation and executive capacity of the agencies of the government responsible for planning, constructing and maintaining the highway system;
(4) the costs of maintenance operations and budgetary provisions for highway maintenance over the past five years, and the present budgetary allocations for highway maintenance;
(5) the highway construction methods at present in use in

the country, the capability of the government and of
local contracting firms to carry out future highway construction, and the current unit costs for constructing
highways (by class, in various types of terrain, including
estimates of the foreign and local currency components
of such costs);

(6) existing legislation regarding the control of motor vehicle
weights and dimensions, highway traffic, and operations
of the highway transport industry (including comment
on the adequacy of such legislation and of its enforcement in relation to highway conditions in the country);

(7) the growth of the motor vehicle fleet in the past ten
years, the existing patterns of vehicle ownership and
usage by main categories, and the cost of vehicle ownership and operation on the existing highway system (by
class of road); and

(8) the major public and private highway transport enterprises and their capacity for providing present and anticipated services in intercity transport.

(c) **Ports and Maritime Transport.** The consultants shall
study the country's ports and the coastal and inland waterways, its
domestic shipping activities, and related transport enterprises, to
assess the future role of maritime transport in the internal distribution system of the country and in foreign trade. The consultants
shall review and analyze:

(1) all available data and reports on port traffic, operations,
finances, administration, terminal facilities, and access
channels of the country's principal ports, of proposed
port installations in these ports and in new port locations;

(2) the present domestic shipping fleet, its capacity, age,
condition, operations and administration; and

(3) the cost of operation and maintenance of ports and of
domestic shipping and the revenues currently derived
from port and shipping operations.

On the basis of the foregoing and the forecasts made in accordance with B-1 of this Section, the consultants shall assess the adequacy of existing and proposed port installations and of the domestic shipping industry, establish the timing for any needed major improvements in ports and domestic shipping, and define the scope of further studies needed prior to their implementation.

(d) Airports and Civil Aviation. The consultants shall study the present status of civil aviation in the country and assess the future role of air transport in domestic and foreign commerce. In this study the consultants shall review and analyze:

(1) the type and age of aircraft in use;
(2) the facilities and conditions at major airports serving civil air traffic;
(3) the organization and management of airports and domestic air carriers;
(4) the cost of operation and maintenance of aircraft and airports; and
(5) the financial condition of domestic air carriers.

On the basis of the above analyses and on forecasts of future traffic demand, the consultants shall identify any shortcomings of the civil aviation industry and the possibilities of improvements in air service and airport facilities. The consultants shall also define the scope of further studies needed prior to implementation of the improvements.

(e) Present Distribution Costs and Transport Policies. Based on the studies of each transport mode outlined in (a) through (d) above, the consultants shall make an analysis of the real cost of distribution by mode (including losses due to delays, inadequate service, and lack of security in transit). The consultants shall also identify the effect of taxes on these costs and of any distortions that may exist due to pricing of foreign exchange, labor, material, or equipment due to public service obligations, or due to government regulations.

To assess the policies of the government in transport pricing, regulation and investment, the consultants shall:

(1) analyze the revenues derived by the government from taxes and user charges on each mode of transport (including that part of license or other fees, taxes and import duties on fuel, spare parts, vehicles, etc., which may appropriately be considered user charges);

(2) determine the adequacy of existing tariffs and user charges to cover the costs of constructing, maintaining and operating each component of the nation's transport system;

(3) summarize and evaluate all existing laws, taxation, licensing and other regulatory measures or practices concerning the operation of each mode of transport;

(4) evaluate the criteria currently in use by the government for making investment decisions in the transport sector; and

(5) examine the organization and operations of each government agency responsible for administration, operation, regulation and planning of transport in the country.

3. *Analysis of Alternative Transport Developments.*

The review and forecast of transport needs and the analyses of the existing transport system outlined in Sections B-1 and B-2 above will result in the identification of a number of possible improvements and extensions of transport services and facilities in the country. The consultants shall evaluate the alternative transport improvements and extensions by analyzing the anticipated economic benefits and costs of new investments required. The economic benefits shall include reductions in transport costs, savings in maintenance costs, and other clearly identifiable benefits; where the development impact of a transport improvement or extension is important, the net value of the additional output shall also be assessed. These calculations shall be made for the economic life of each investment, on the basis of broad estimates of benefits and costs.

To estimate the investments required (in both physical and financial terms) in 1969-73 for the recommended transport improvements and extensions, the consultants shall determine the following:

(a) For railways—
  (1) the operational and design standards for each new or improved section of line (including track, signalling, and requirements for terminals, yard and workshop facilities);
  (2) the future equipment requirements (including type and number of locomotives, rolling stock, and maintenance equipment); and
  (3) any auxiliary requirements for new facilities (administration, communications, training, etc.).
(b) For highways and highway transport—
  (1) the design standards to be assigned to each highway (design speed, roadway and pavement width, pavement type, maximum grades, minimum radii, design loads, and structure clearances);
  (2) the sections of new highways to be constructed and of existing highways to be maintained or improved (cost estimates to be based on current mileage costs applicable to the selected standard and category of terrain);
  (3) the new highway maintenance equipment and shops required and the annual costs of highway maintenance;
  (4) the type and number of additional vehicles required to provide a satisfactory level of service; and
  (5) the public and private terminals, shops, and auxiliary facilities required to operate and maintain the additional vehicles.
(c) For ports and maritime transport—
  (1) the navigation channel and harbor basin improvements (including approximate extent of breakwater construction, depths and quantities of dredging, navigational aids, harbor tugs and pilot vessels);
  (2) new terminal construction (including area of land reclamation, berth construction, moorings, type and size of cargo transit and storage facilities, cargo handling equipment, and provisions for truck and/or rail access);
  (3) vessel requirements for domestic shipping (including type and number of self-propelled vessels and/or barges and tugs); and

70

    (4) requirements for new auxiliary port installations (port maintenance equipment and shop facilities, ship repair and bunkering facilities, administration, emergency equipment, training, etc.).

(d) For airports and civil aviation—

    (1) the location and type of new or improved landing facilities (including length, width and type of surfacing for runways, taxiways and aprons, lighting, air traffic control, equipment and other navigational aids);

    (2) new terminal building construction (including type and size of passenger and freight terminals, hangars, shop facilities, and related equipment requirements);

    (3) new aircraft requirements (number, type and general characteristics of flight equipment) ; and

    (4) any requirements for auxiliary air transport facilities (administration, fueling and emergency equipment, training, etc.).

4. *Recommended Transport Investments and their Financing.*

Based an the analysis outlined in Section B-3 above, the consultants shall determine the relative priorities of new investments in transport and prepare specific recommendations for transport development. The program for the first five years (1969-73) shall be worked out in detail; for the subsequent years (1974-83) it shall be in more general form and consist of (a) estimates of expenditures which would be incurred after 1973 from investments initiated before then; (b) projects which were reviewed and found not justified for execution in 1969-73, but which appear justified thereafter; and (c) global estimates of expenditure trends for transportation. These recommendations shall comprise an optimum program to serve the country's transport needs. The investment program shall be given in both physical and financial terms. To the extent possible, the government will advise the consultants regarding the order of magnitude of total resources that will become available for public investment in the transport sector in 1969-73 and in 1974-83. The recommended programs shall define the general scope of the proposed improvements for each mode, give the time schedule for implementation of each improvement, and provide estimates of the foreign and local currency cost components.

The consultants shall also study alternative sources of financing the proposed investment program and make recommendations as to the most appropriate methods of financing. For this purpose, they should review the level of revenues from charges on the users of transport services (whether earmarked or not) and make forecasts for the railway and other major public entities of revenues (including user charges) and expenditures to indicate to what extent they will be able to finance proposed investments from these sources; if such financing appears inadequate, they should consider the desirability of increasing tariffs or other user charges.

5. *Recommended Government Policies.*

The consultants shall prepare an outline of government policies and measures necessary to (a) implement the recommended program of new investments in the transport sector and (b) obtain the maximum economic benefits from both the existing transport infrastructure and from the proposed improvements. This shall include recommendations on:

(1) the formulation of appropriate criteria on which to base future investment and disinvestment decisions;

(2) the establishment of rates and fares on government-owned transport enterprises which reflect transport costs;

(3) the establishment of user charges applicable to private transport enterprises which reflect the cost to the government of constructing, maintaining and operating highways, ports, airports and related facilities;

(4) the establishment of policies concerning taxation and other fiscal measures, public service obligations, credit availability, etc., which are neutral, i.e. do not discriminate as between the various modes;

(5) the establishment, abandonment, continuation or modification of administrative and tariff regulations relating to private and public transport enterprises;

(6) the improvements needed in the organization of existing

72

agencies responsible for administration, operation, regulation and planning in each mode of transport, and/or the formation of new agencies to perform these functions; and

(7) the organizational requirements needed to develop and implement on a continuing basis coordinated transport policies and planning, including definition of the type of organization that would be appropriate and viable, the extent of its authority, and its financial and staffing requirements.

6. *Advisory Services and Training.*

The consultants shall identify major areas in the field of transportation planning in which (a) advisory services could be most usefully provided to the government for a total period of two man-years, and (b) further training abroad would be most useful to nationals of the country working in transportation. It is proposed to provide four man-years of such training.

C. *Reports and Time Schedule*

The consultants shall commence field work within thirty calendar days of the effective date of this contract. They shall submit the following reports within the time periods indicated, beginning on the effective date of the contract:

(1) an Inception Report (10 copies) summarizing their initial findings within three months;

(2) Progress Reports (10 copies) at two-month intervals after the Inception Report, giving a statement of all work performed during the reporting period, a summary of interim findings, and the schedule of work for the next reporting period;

(3) by July 31 and January 31 of each year, a Statistical Supplement showing personnel employed, equipment ordered and delivered, and sub-contracts entered into for the preceding periods of January 1 to June 30 and July 1 to December 31, respectively;

(4) a Draft Final Report on the transport survey (20 copies), summarizing all work performed, the findings and recommendations of the consultants, and giving maps, plans and diagrams of the proposed transport program, within ten months; and

(5) a Final Report or Reports (number of copies to be determined by the government and the Bank) incorporating all revisions deemed appropriate by the consultants after receipt of comments on the Draft Final Report from the government and the Bank, within forty-five days of receipt of comments.

The reports shall contain a concise summary of all major findings and recommendations of the consultants. The estimates of costs and benefits and all economic analyses which support the consultants' conclusions shall be presented in sufficient detail to permit checking of all calculations without supplementary data. The Draft Final Report shall be carefully edited and complete, so that production of the Final Reports can proceed without delay.

III. DATA, LOCAL SERVICES AND FACILITIES TO BE PROVIDED BY THE GOVERNMENT

A. Economic, Traffic and Technical Data

The government will provide the consultants with all available data on:

(1) the country's economic development program, including the distribution of population and the location of agricultural, mining and industrial production and consumption;

(2) traffic by all modes of transport;

(3) an inventory of highways;

(4) maps of the country and its transport networks;

(5) cost experience on recent construction projects; and

(6) the estimated opportunity cost of capital in the country.

74

The government will also furnish the consultants with all available information on transport costs and revenues and on the organization, operation and accounting system of the government agencies responsible for transport administration.

B. *Cooperation of Governmental Agencies and Counterparts*

In connection with work by the consultants that requires the cooperation of other government agencies, the government will provide liaison and will ensure that the consultants have access to all information required for the completion of the services.

The government will assign qualified counterparts to work with the key personnel of the consultants. The counterparts will be assigned on a full-time basis for the purpose of liaison, training and review of the findings and recommendations of the consultants.

C. *Facilities and Supporting Staff*

The government will provide the following facilities and staff to help the consultants in performing the services:

(1) office space, furniture, equipment and office supplies;
(2) administrative, interpreter and translator, secretarial and clerical services including printing and computer service;
(3) professional or technical services;
(4) transportation within the country; and
(5) utilities, telephone, postage, telex and telegraph services.

BIBLIOGRAPHY

The literature on transportation in developing countries is most inadequate and not a single publication deals comprehensively with sector and project planning. However, those who may wish to pursue the subject further may find the following suggestions helpful; a particularly useful bibliography can be found in Fromm's *Transport Investment and Economic Development* listed below.

Hans A. Adler, *Economic Appraisal of Transport Projects: A Manual with Case Studies*, Indiana University Press, Bloomington and London, 1971.

Robert T. Brown, *Transport and the Economic Integration of South America*, The Brookings Institution, Washington, D.C., 1966.

M. L. Burstein and others, *The Cost of Trucking*, Northwestern University, Evanston, Illinois, 1965.

G. Charlesworth and J. L. Paisley, "The Economic Assessments of Returns from Road Works," *Proceedings of the Institution of Civil Engineers*, London, November 1959.

Jan de Weille, "Quantification of Road User Savings," *World Bank Staff Occasional Papers No. 2*, Washington, D.C., 1966.

Gary Fromm (editor), *Transport Investment and Economic Development*, The Brookings Institution, Washington, D.C., 1965.

Clell G. Harral, *Preparation and Appraisal of Transport Projects*, The Brookings Institution, Washington, D.C., 1965.

E. K. Hawkins, "Investment in Roads in Underdeveloped Countries," *Bulletin of the Oxford University Institute of Statistics,* November 1960.

E. K. Hawkins, *Roads and Road Transport in an Underdeveloped Country: A Case Study of Uganda,* H. M. Stationery Office, London, 1962.

V. W. Hogg and C. M. Roelandts, *Nigerian Motor Vehicle Traffic, An Economic Forecast,* London, 1962.

B. V. Martin and C. B. Warden, *Transportation Planning in Developing Countries,* The Brookings Institution, Washington, D.C., 1965.

R. S. Millard and R. S. P. Bonney, "The Costs of Operating Buses and Trucks on Roads with Different Surfaces in Africa," *Road International,* June 1965.

H. Mohring and M. Harwitz, *Highway Benefits, An Analytical Framework,* Northwestern University, Evanston, Illinois, 1962.

Lionel Odier, *The Economic Benefits of Road Construction and Improvements,* Publications ESTOUP, Paris, 1963.

Wilfred Owen, *Strategy for Mobility,* The Brookings Institution, Washington, D.C., 1964.

E. E. Pollack, "Methods Currently Used in Calculating Direct Savings in Transport Costs and the Indirect Social Economic Benefits Derived from Road Improvement Projects," *Transport and Communications Bulletin No. 37,* ECAFE, 1964.

A. R. Prest and R. Turvey, "Cost Benefit Analysis: A Survey," *Economic Journal,* December, 1965.

Herman G. van der Tak and Jan de Weille, "Reappraisal of a Road Project in Iran," *World Bank Staff Occasional Papers No. 7,* Washington, D.C., 1969.

G. W. Wilson, B. R. Bergmann, L. V. Hirsch, and M. S. Klein, *The Impact of Highway Investment on Development,* The Brookings Institution, Washington, D.C., 1966.

David M. Winch, *The Economics of Highway Planning,* Toronto, 1962.